Investing For Kids +
Gardening for Kids

2 in 1 Kids Training Value Pack
The No 1 Kids Pack to Learn how to Earn, Save, Invest,
Grow Money, and Learn all about Gardening

By Daphne M Cooper

This book belongs to

____

Table of Contents

My other books you will love! 136

Don't forget to grab your GIFT!!!...137

Investing For kids

Learn how to start Earning, Saving, Investing, and watch your money grow

By Daphne M Cooper

Just for You

A free gift to our readers

Click here

http://daphnemcooper.com/parenting.pdf

Joining the PME Community

Looking to meet other parents that can help you on your parenting journey? If so, then check out the Parenting Made Easy (PME) Community here:

https://www.facebook.com/groups/293830159257919/

Introduction

Whenever the word investing, money or finances are mentioned, you may think it is boring. But it is certainly not boring to go shopping for shoes, toys or candy. Whizzing down the aisle, it is so fun to look at everything available, and I can bet there are quite a few things you wouldn't mind buying. But to buy items that cost more than the money you currently have in your pocket; you may need to learn a thing or two. This is why I am here to help!

Learning about finances does NOT have to be boring. It does NOT have to be complicated. And it does NOT have to be confusing or difficult. Many things in this world are just over-complicated and people tend to do that. Words are used to make facts fly over people's heads (much like Peter Pan flying to Neverland). And when you do not understand words, it is also just no fun. But here, every big word is explained, simplified and examples will be given, allowing you to picture it in your head.

Can I Earn Money?

What if there is a way you can learn to earn money? What if you can put your money in a certain place, and watch it grow? Much like planting a seed in a pot and

watching it sprout? Well, it is possible! This is called investing, and the truth about investing is that you can start at almost any age. Time can be your enemy, but it can also be your ally (Zig Ziglar Quotes). The younger you start investing, the better! Then you are friends with time, as you have plenty of it! Plenty of time to learn that sometimes putting money away can result in receiving more money a little while later. If you receive more money, you can buy something bigger and better than what you first could! (Tara Siegel, 2020).

To learn how to invest, you will have to know the basics of money. Don't worry, you won't get bored to death! Think of it this way - You are a gold miner, looking for that nugget of gold. But if you waltz into the cave, what do you think will happen?

Well, firstly, you won't be able to see anything. You do not have a torch! You will stumble about blindly. You won't even know where to go. Consider this book your torch. It lights your way to your golden nugget, but to add a bonus, I will also provide you with the tools. There is no way you are mining that gold from the rock with your bare hands. You will need a pickaxe, maybe a drill, and even wooden beams to keep the mine from falling. All this will take time (much like investing), but soon you will see a growth in the amount of money you have.

Isn't Making Money for Grownups?

It is the grownup's primary responsibility to earn money, but that does not mean you cannot learn how to! The sooner you learn, the better, because it will help you now and long into the future. I bet you have learned about habits. How good habits help you in life, and how bad habits make life hard. Learning good habits with money, learning about investing, is such an incredibly good habit that you will be forever grateful for learning it! (Booth, 2020)

And do you know what the coolest part of it all is? You are probably learning something that very few of your friends are learning! If you like competitions, consider yourself a step ahead in the game. This is because schools barely cover any of this! They focus on other subjects (such as maths, languages, and science), which although good for your education, are not so beneficial for your current piggy bank. Learning how to invest, grow your money and other matters are needed in everyday life, but schools barely brush on the topic. You will see for yourself as time goes by and you advance in grades. Again, this puts you a step ahead in the game, and everyone will be wondering why you are so savvy and wise before you even hit college!

Not Everything is THAT Easy Right?

Well, in truth, no. Some matters can be a little more difficult to grasp than others, but any difficult term or words will be explained. Any issues, rules, and subjects when it comes to investing and making money will be simplified for you, and you will not walk alone in this journey. This book will guide you every step of the way. Do not be afraid to take your time with this, read things slowly, and make sure you understand each chapter before you move on. Take notes, have fun! Try to explain things to an adult. You will find that you remember a lot more once you have to teach someone else about it. So don't hesitate to share what you have learned!

A good idea would be to work through this with a grownup. Not only can the adult brush up on some of the facts, but they can also help you apply the principles in your everyday life. Whether it be finding a good place to invest, setting money aside, and making sure you don't spend it when you shouldn't. It may also mean that they will start to learn to invest with you, making it a fun bonding time with your family member!

So, you don't have to worry, you are covered. You have the toolkit to start investing, as well as learn principles in finances that most people only learn once they receive their first paycheck. You will also have time, a valuable commodity that adults do not normally have. The more you use your time wisely, the better (perhaps even opening up time for yourself in the future).

So don't be afraid to start today, one chapter at a time. With a little bit of fun, a little bit of magic, and a little bit of work, watch your knowledge grow, and your money increase.

About The Author

Being a mother, investing is a very important aspect I am adding to my children's lives. Guiding them with this step-by-step method to prepare them for a better and brighter future. The techniques are simple and easy, and I want to share them with you just as I have shared them with my children.

I want you to make the most of your childhood, and with my knowledge and guidance, you will find yourself sailing through many of the facts. You will grow in your knowledge of money, how to grow it and how to have fun while doing it! Sure, there is not a lot of charm or sparkles that comes with money, but watching it grow, seeing your success, and being able to buy or save up for something that you want is by far an amazing feeling. Especially if you manage to conquer this on your own.

I have walked this journey with my children, and I hope to walk this journey with you. So don't hesitate! Start reading and discovering the amazing secrets of investing today.

Chapter 1: Understanding Money

Today we will be talking a little bit about money. After all, there is more to it than handing a couple of dollar bills to someone in exchange for food or toys, or gadgets. To understand money, you just have to dig a little deeper. Consider this as the first step into discovering the gold nuggets hidden deep within the cave.

Now before we continue, there is just one thing you need to understand. Money can be both a terrible and a wonderful thing. It depends entirely on your approach to getting it. It can either be your master or it can be your servant. Which one do you believe is better?

If you prefer it to be your servant, you are correct. Because money is an excellent servant, but a terrible master (Barnum, Forbes). Therefore, you need to promise now at the very beginning that you will not let money control you. Money is not a supervillain in a movie, but in real life, it may as well be. There are many cases where people have done extremely bad things for money. However, those people (being the superhero of finances) thrived and decided to make money their servant. So now that you understand that money can be both good and bad, let us take a look at the role money plays in people's lives - including yours!

What is Money?

So what exactly is money? In simplest terms, it is a form of exchange. You exchange a certain amount of money for a laptop, or even something as simple as a bag of apples. Money is used to discover the value of something. After all, people do not fight so hard in competitions unless 1 million dollars was worth something to them.

Money allows you to buy things, whether it be online or at the shops, but to buy items with money - you will need to get money in the first place. Normally, your parents give you money (or you work for it), but at the end of the day, where do your parents get your money?

Apparently, your parents work for it! Do you know why people need to work for money? Well, in the olden days, people used to trade and barter. This meant that people traded their skills or products for others (Anderson, 2021). This is all good and well, except if you want to trade a table for some bread. How would this work? The table has more value than bread, but you cannot just chop a table in pieces. Now, normally a system could get set up where the baker owes bread for the table for the next three weeks. As this matter is unreliable, the written value system was established where traders used to write values on a piece of paper. People accept these values, and that was the creation of money. It was meant to solve the differences in value **for different services and products! Now isn't** that neat?

The Importance of Money

This brings back the question of how important money is. Well, to answer this question, it is best to ask, what exactly can money do for you? A good example is to think why pirates spent their lives in dangerous seas hunting for treasure? Well, naturally, it can have them buy a better ship, it can let them buy land, it can let them buy better weapons, etc. So now it is best to ask the question:

What Can Money Do for You Even as A Kid?

Money gives you a lot of freedom. This is clear for both kids and adults. Money allows you to do things that you want, where you want and whenever you want. Enough money can even allow you to leave a job you sorely dislike and you do not have to rely on anyone else for financial support. And as you are younger, money can help support your hobbies, your education and other matters that you may enjoy. For example, if you are an artist, you need some money for a pencil and paper. If you want to play the guitar, then you need money to buy the instrument and guitar lessons. If you want to go to school, then you need money to pay for the school.

Money can also give you choices

Nothing is more fun than being able to choose something that you want. Just choose flavor ice cream, or whether or not you want to visit someone. Having the choices is truly the best feeling in the whole wide world. But if you are stuck, and have no money, you can see your options slowly but surely getting less and less. That is no fun at all; many adults dread this very thought. So, if you have the options, it can come as a great relief.

When you have enough money, you should choose what you usually want or do not want to do. When you are older, if you want to change or quit your job, it would be good to have money for survival. If you want to travel to different countries - then the money is a must. If you want to go on vacation and buy yourself ice cream at the seaside, that costs money too.

Money gives you financial security

This may or may not be a strange idea. It is scary to think about whether or not you have money, but there are chances you do know a little of what it actually feels like. Financial security just reduces a lot of the stress in a person's life as well as your relationship with your family. Having money can lift a massive burden. You may not have to pay bills today, but when you get older, you will understand that money can help you pay the bill as well as provide security that you know when your next meal is coming (All4kids, 2021).

Having money just makes life easier for a family, as financial security can remove a lot of stress in people's lives.

Money can allow you to have more fun

Everyone knows you need money to experience a lot of fun things in life. Riding on a rollercoaster or taking a hike at the park. Money can truly allow you to experience the best of things. Whether or not it is getting a fancy  PlayStation or even going on a trip to the zoo! You can experience a lot of what life has to offer. This is sad, but a somewhat helpful tip about the day and age we now live in.

Money can also allow your family to give more

Money can teach you how to learn good living and work ethic. Many people who do not necessarily spoil their children in riches, but teach them how to work for it, allow them to forge their path into a wealthier life (Hayes, 2021). Many parents send their children to school with barely any money with this in mind. Education gives you the great opportunity to learn how to earn money.

That is why it is so important to study for those tests! They are not there to make your life miserable. They are there to allow you to learn how to earn money. It may seem odd but learning how to work out maths gives you a great advantage when you work on your finances later in life! Learning about biology can get you an education as a scientist and a nice paycheck.

Keep in mind, it is best to choose a career for yourself in the future that you will enjoy. That will give you the motivation to work harder and earn more. So, take your time during your school years to discover what you enjoy. It will get you very far.

Money does allow you to give back

At a certain point and time in your life, you can even learn to give back to those who do not have the money. Especially if you start earning money a lot sooner and a lot younger. You can help a local charity or even a certain cause which you would like to support. Great happiness comes from lending a helping hand to people who are less fortunate than you (Santi, 2017). Who knows, you may even inspire others to follow in your footsteps. That sounds a lot like being a superhero, doesn't it?

Dark Side of Money

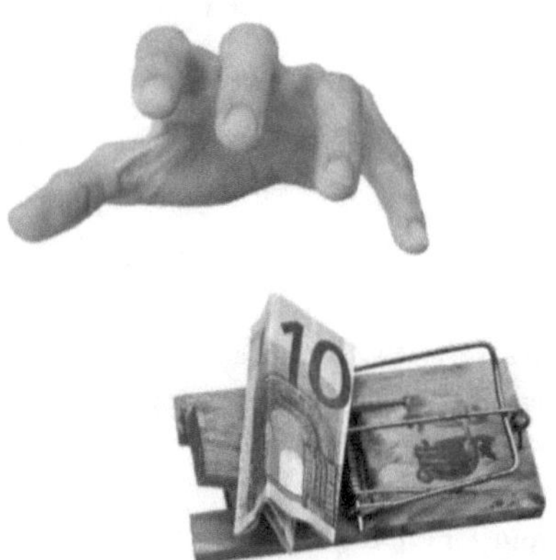

Unfortunately, in every story, there is a villain. The same can be said for the money. You can use the money for so much good. For yourself, your family, and your community. But remember that sometimes there are a few bad things that come along with money.

You have to be very careful! Especially at your age, it may be hard to realize. But as you grow older, it will become more and more obvious how people have been affected by the dark side of money. This is when people allow money to be their master and they be its servant. We do not want that, oh no! Remember! You are the master of money, not the other way around! You control the crown, and the throne, and it must remain so! Here are some common warning signs of an attack on the dark side of money!

First of all, money obsession can cause problems. This happens when money is all people can think about. You cannot get away from it. People who try to search for money and think about it all the time will just bring trouble and problems into their

lives. It will cause them to do things they shouldn't do, and to fail in other matters where they shouldn't fail (Carlson, 2021).

When money is all that, you are thinking about, then you know you are doing something wrong. You can focus on earning money or learning about it. But make sure it is not what you are always thinking about getting. Remember, the more obsessed you are, the more bad things could happen. So, although it is good to think about money and what it can do for you, take a step back and think, "Is money controlling me? Or am I controlling it?" It should be quite easy to get an answer. Even if it is from you or the thoughts of others. The point is, if you obsess too much over money, you are not going to enjoy life.

Making money can cause more stress. This is what you need to be very careful about even at your age. Even if you lose money, do not let it bring you down. Money can bring some unwanted stress for people who believe that they are not getting enough money and they should always have more. This is the kind of thinking people have when they gamble. Most of the time, they will lose their money then (helpguidewp et al., 2021).

Start thinking about it like this: be happy with what you have and see what you can improve. Simple & Easy! You want to earn money because you want to learn how to work with finances. You want to learn to invest because you want to see the money grow. It must not be forced, and do not form a second thought that you need more. If you have a bed to sleep in, food to eat, and clothes to wear as well as education, then you have enough. So, by the end of the day, you want to earn money because you can, and it is the wise thing to do. It is not because you have to, because as of right now, depending on where you are in life, you do not have that pressure just quite yet. This makes it easier for you to control money. After all, if you lose it, it is not the end of the world. You can learn from your mistakes and try again.

How Much Money Is Enough?

This is a good question. A lot of people just think 1 million dollars! Others may consider that having enough money to pay the bills is ok. For you that is just starting, any money that you have is enough. After all, you are learning how to use the money. You do not need the pressure of what will happen if I do not earn enough? At least, not yet anyway.

Again, it is great to set a goal to see if you can reach it. If you have 5 dollars in your pocket, buy some candy and sell it at school, then you have $20. It may not be enough to buy a cell phone, but it is certainly enough for you right now. Because you have learned how to earn an extra $15. Then if you decide to grow and expand that is up to you. But even now, do not let your love of money cause you to:

- Hurt people - this is the first rule of the game. You are forbidden to be mean!
- Move away from good friends and family - do not cut yourself off from anyone, especially people who can help you walk this journey!
- Take too much time out of your studies.
- Take too much time from your family.
- Sacrifice your time to enjoy normal activities and sports.

To bring back the example of a miner, you normally never mine on your own. You have a buddy to come with you. If your buddy tells you that you are going too deep, or it is getting too dangerous. What is the best thing you can do? Well, that is to pull back of course! You don't want to get hurt when digging for gold. The same can be said for money. You do not want to get hurt while learning how to work with money. Otherwise, a game that was once fun is now spoiled. And this relies entirely upon your attitude of what you want to do and learn.

Rather, follow the instructions that are given to you. Even if you only mine a small nugget at first, you at least now know how to mine. When you get older, you can focus on going a little deeper without having that fear of safety. The same can be said about money. You can learn a lot about money now, which will help you in the future. Imagine being able to make more money than your friends before you even hit college! Isn't that just amazing?

Not All Happiness Relies on Money

This is just a good reminder here and now that not all happiness relies on how much money you can make (Dunn & Courtney, 2021). Of course, it is good to have financial goals at your age. It is perfect to learn how to make your budget. It is fantastic to grow the amount of money you have. This is never a bad thing!

But then again, don't get addicted to the idea that money can buy you happiness. Your family and friends should remain important. Remember, you have time to learn how to make money, and you do not have such excessive pressure of failing. So this is a good time to learn how to make money, but you never, ever want to let money have a massive impact on you. I'm gonna say it again, and you are going to say it with me:

Money Is a Great Servant. Money Is a Terrible Master!

If there is anything you can and should learn from this chapter, it is this fact. Because money can do a lot for you. That part is obvious. Money plays an important role in many people's lives. That is also a fact. But allowing yourself to be the superhero rather than the villain when it comes to money is your choice. So, which one will you choose? The right side, or the dark side?

Furthermore, do not be afraid of what you can and cannot do. There may be many suggestions, and it would be best to ask an adult to try these activities. After all, if you do not understand something, or are a little scared to try it out on your own, it is best to have someone with you that has spent time and hours working with money.

Making money is not necessarily easy. Investing is not easy either, but learning from the start can truly boost your success in the future. Worries about overspending and not being able to meet your bills will become a matter of the past.

Chapter 2: History of Money

So naturally, there is a start to everything right? A chicken comes from an egg for example. There was the start of a paper airplane too. Someone folded a piece of paper with hopes that it would fly into the air. There is even a beginning of a computer, and cell phones. Everything has a beginning, and the same can be said for money. So how exactly did money begin? Now that is a very good question. Well, money started to solve a problem, and we will be looking at that in-depth with this chapter.

Where it First Started

Money can be anything. It can be represented by that of a metal coin, a piece of paper (what you may be familiar with), or even something as simple as a shell! So tell me, why do you think that you can trade a couple of shells for a loaf of bread?

Well, that is because people place value on it! It is used as a form of exchange and allows people to choose the value of their items and services. For instance, a loaf of bread is going to be cheaper than television. How do you know that? Well, because of the amount of money it costs! Do you think you can buy a television with the same amount of money as a loaf of bread? Of course not! That is just silly! But this allows you to see that money has value because people believe that it does - which is why money works all too well.

But throughout history, you can imagine that money has changed. We aren't carrying around our bags of gold to buy a house. Nor taking seashells to our grocery store. Things have changed over time, and to appreciate money, it is best to take a deep look into its history. Don't be afraid! It is quite an easy journey and fun facts that you can share with your friends. Now you can truly answer the question of: where did money come from?

Believe it or not, money has been in existence for the last 3,000 years (Beattie, 2021). That means the idea and invention of money is over 3,000 years old! That is how many great-grandfathers for you? Don't worry, you don't need to figure that one out.

But before the money had been used so many years ago, there was likely to be a system of bartering. However, keep in mind, this is a guess...a logical guess, but still a guess from historians. What are historians? People who study history and work out what happened in the past. They are the ones who believed that bartering was used before money. And it does make sense.

What is Bartering?

Bartering happens when you trade a good or service for another good or service. For example, you trade your cow's milk for some eggs. Or you can specifically exchange a bushel of grain for a pair of shoes. But whenever these arrangements are made, they would take an immense amount of time. For example, if you had an axe you wanted to trade for some meat and skin of a mammoth, you  would search and find someone who would be willing to take the axe and help hunt down this enormous creature. However, if the people do not like this deal, then you may want to change the deal, adding more for what they believe to be worth the risk (Corporate Finance Institute, 2021).

Over time, history has shown that different currencies (forms of money) were starting to grow. It normally involved items that could very easily be traded to and through, such as salt, weapons, and animal skins. This developed over time as more and more people started making discoveries. Naturally, a wooden spear turned into a spear with an iron tip, etc. These items were good forms of exchange, but how valuable they were to a person was still relatively debatable.

When Money was introduced, it rapidly increased the speed of transactions. You know how long it can take standing at a till waiting for your turn to pay. Now imagine, some of these trades could very well take hours, to even days depending on the situation!

What Was The First Form of Money?

In 1,200 BC Cowrie Shells - a shell of a prominent and widely available mollusk was used as money - specifically in China in the period of the Shang Dynasty. The beauty of the shells was its near impossibility to forge them (after all, who could go out and create a shell?) However, the shell was not just used in China, but

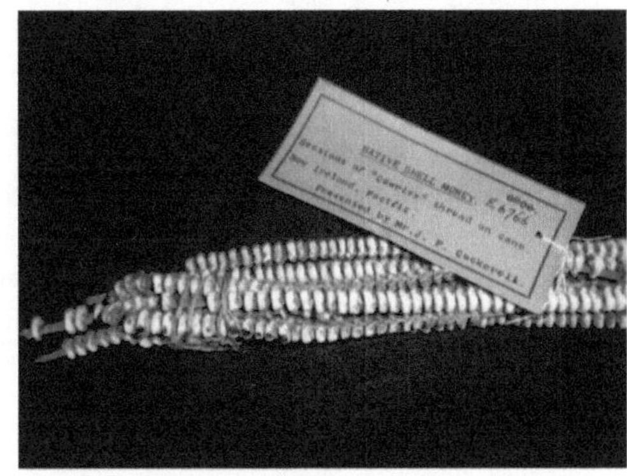

other societies in Africa and even India made use of the cowries. This is because it was used the longest, and many people used them! It may as well have been as popular then as the US dollar is today! Imagine that! Money out of seashells! Do you think you could carry around a bunch of seashells in exchange for some food or toys? (Honick, 2021)

When Did Money Become Metal?

The cowrie shells acted as an inspiration. China started to create bronze as well as copper cowrie shell look-alikes in 1000 BC. This could be considered as one of the very earliest forms of metal coins. They then developed into round coins - the base was completely made of metal and even contained holes so that they could be strung together like a chain (NOVA Online, n.d.).

Taking a peek outside of China, many Greek cities of Iona started designing coins for the use of the business. The place that started it all was called Sardis which was the capital city of Lydia (or what you now know as Turkey!) And believe it or not, the coins looked a lot like the coins we know and see today! (Honick, 2021)

Naturally, once one thing was invented, as time passed by, more and more people wanted to develop and change it for the better. This is especially true of the great empires that ruled the world - Greek, Persia, even Macedonia, and Rome. The coins had an image of the different gods they had served or emperors who had ruled in to act as a mark of authenticity. (Because even in that time people tried to make fake money! Therefore, it was best to make the coins hard to forge.)

In 118 BC - China started to create leather money. Leather money was made from white deerskin and could be considered as the very first banknote ever. One of these deerskins was as valuable as 40,000 'cash' or a metal coin (Honick, 2021).

Source: Sutori

The Growth in The Rest of The World

Many areas of Europe still consistently used metal coins as the only means of payments and currencies dating up to the late 16th century. This is because they got possession of many new territories, allowing them to gain constant sources of precious metals - making coins still an easy accessory (Beattie, 2021).

However, lugging around so many coins for far travels was not only impractical but also very unsafe. Banks were created, where they designed paper notes. People could place their money in the bank for exchange of such papers and come back any time to the bank for exchange of metal coins again. Or even the paper money itself could be used to buy certain goods as well as services. It was far more practical and safe. A person had a lot less to carry, and the government was now responsible for the issuing of most currencies.

Currency Wars

Well, history is full of wars, there was even something called a currency war. This is because paper money allowed international trade (buying items all over the world) to start. However, other countries had different forms of currencies. This meant that one currency had a different value over another. Countries would compete, trying to change the value of the enemy's currencies by driving it down or reducing the ability to buy for the other country. This caused certain countries to have to change their currency (Picardo, 2019).

As you may now be aware, not everything can be paid for in dollars. There are still many other currencies in the world. For example, in the UK, there is the pound. In India, it's the rupee, and in South Korea, it's the Won.

How Does Money Work Now?

You probably have worked with cellphones and computers before. Life is becoming more digital, and cash is starting to decrease. Rather, money is starting to change into virtual currency. You can pay for goods and services on your phone for example or even a credit card. So many payments can be done in a virtual way that you do not even have to carry cash around with you to make a payment!

There has even been a creation of digital coins such as Bitcoins, but we will not be diving in too deep, as cryptocurrency should never be considered as a proper form of investment - especially not for children.

At The End of The Day

Money still plays a huge role in this age. Now you know how it started. How it changed, and you know in what forms it can come today. You will likely deal with virtual money rather than real money (unless you are selling items at a flea market). When it comes to investing and investments, most of it is done on a digital basis, and you will have to learn to work with a computer or be assisted by an adult. Keep in mind this very important rule...this rule most people do not follow, but should:

Do not spend any money that you cannot afford to lose. Now, this may be difficult to apply if you don't need to worry too much about money. But this very important rule will save your life in the future. So, remember this line, memorize it, and keep thinking about it as time moves on.

Chapter 3: Earning Money

So is it possible to earn money at this age? Yes! Absolutely! The best part about the day and age you live in is the fact that a computer and internet connection paired with some knowledge is all you need to kick start earning an income. Does it make it easy? No, it comes with hard work and dedication, but by the end of the day, almost anyone is now capable of earning money, regardless of age. And to start learning how to invest, it may be a good idea to earn some extra money.

But before we start with all the ideas, it is best to take one last look at how far money has truly come. We have brushed on the history of money in the previous chapter, but more on a matter of how money was created. Now we will be taking a peek at the timeline:

Timeline of Money

In the Bronze Age of the year 3000 B.C, money was starting to become a commodity. This means that money was created out of objects that had worth. This added to the authenticity as well as a more widespread form of exchange. For example, the use of cowry shells (Beattie, 2021).

China started to make miniature replicas around 1100 B.C where you could design bronze replicas of items that were already of

use. To get a sword, you would need to have a miniature bronze equivalent of a sword to get one. This was, however, quite impractical, because having to carry around so many objects made you a target, added to your burden of travels, and far more likely to get killed for your money (Philosopher's Library, n.d.).

The first official currency that has been recorded was the Lydian Lion around the year 600 B.C. As mentioned before, this is now where modern Turkey now resides. King Alyattes had the coins minted, and it is the first official currency that has ever been proved. There is a likelihood that there had been currencies before theirs, but so much evidence of history has been lost this will be incredibly hard to discover (Beattie, 2021).

Then in 700 A.D in the Tang Dynasty of China, paper money came into existence. The government had realized the need for lighter loads to perform bigger transactions. However, there was a message on some of them, "If you fake it we will cut your head,"- for anyone who tries to forge them. This is quite a serious threat they gave to criminals.

In the year 1200 A.D, paper notes arrived due to the travels of the incredible explorer Marco Polo. However, until the year 1661, the first Banknote was issued in Sweden (Beattie, 2021).

The US Dollar was then invented in 1792, on April the 2nd. This is when the coins and notes officially came to life in the United States of America. From March 3, 1933, to

August 15, 1971, President Franklin D Roosevelt had all the banks in the U.S.A closed. This was because of the run at gold reserves. This was because the banks held a lot of the

gold which was used in the exchange for U.S dollars, and there was a certain fixed exchange rate between the two (Blessing, 2020).

When the president made this bold move, he banned the ability to exchange dollars for gold for a short period. Then he made an order for Americans to turn and exchange the gold they had for U.S dollars. This move allowed Fort Knox to now have the largest supply of gold globally and fully pushed the citizens to use American dollars rather than gold. They also made dollars dependent on currencies rather than gold (Wikipedia contributors, 2021).

In 1946, the first bank card was issued. This was all under a program of "Charge-It" where the idea was a merchant could send the sales slip into the bank and the bank would pay them and charge the customer (Charge It, 2017).

In 1950, Frank McNamara designed a card that could allow you to dine in restaurants, and the Diners club would pay your bill. Afterward, you would repay them later. It was originally designed for a small group of people, but the idea caught on like wildfire, and within a year there were about 20,000 cardholders! (History and Legacy, n.d.)

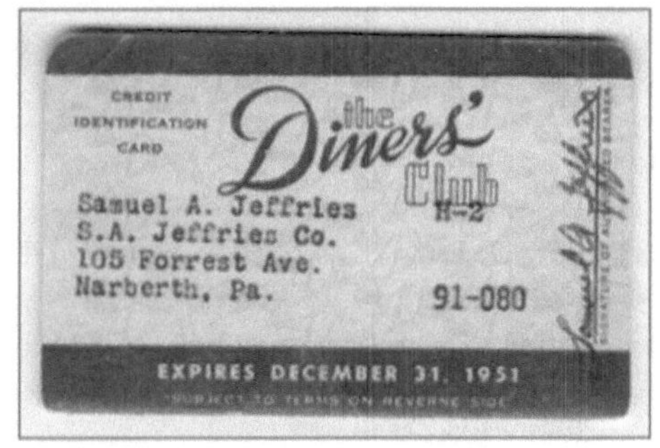

In 1990, PayPal and digital money came to being. PayPal changed the world for the better, allowing you to make payments from a computer to another computer in a matter of seconds. In 2009, Bitcoin and cryptocurrencies had started (Philosopher's Library, n.d.).

How can I Earn Money?

So now that you understand which way the world is heading, it is best to consider digital and physical options in matters of earning some extra cash. After all, it is far safer to stay at home and easier than to set up a lemonade stand outside and hope to sell something in that manner.

Washing Cars

Let us start with an age-old job that can get you some extra cash without much stress. Many people do not have the time to wash their cars as it takes a lot of time and can get very messy. So, there is always a major job opportunity there! A great way to get started is to advertise on social media, or with an adult, go door to door to offer your services. It may seem scary at first, but once you get used to it, you will be doing yourself a major favor! (Bell, 2021)

Becoming an Influencer

If you like being in front of a camera, and your parents don't mind, then this is a classic and great way to start earning money! This takes a lot of time and effort, but in reality, those are two things you have right now. So, keep building your following until you are officially able to  monetize the accounts you have. You do, however, have to be 13 years or older to sign up on most platforms. Even Instagram and Tik Tok are really good ways to build an audience and make some extra cash too (Kultkid, 2019).

Becoming a Streamer

If you are into video games, then streaming is certainly the way to go! This is how adults are making a living - doing something they love? So why not set up and start now? Streamers do make money by selling subscriptions, displaying ads as well as working with brands. All you need to do is build your viewership (Bell, 2021).

Sell Stuff At A Farmers Market

Whether it is your freshly baked chocolate brownies or your beautiful hand-crafted bracelets, take advantage of farmers' markets nearby to start your own little business! You can even grow fruits and veggies to sell or create homemade jams. All these items normally sell well at higher prices (Nationwide, 2021).

Mowing Lawns

An age-old job that still needs doing now and then. It is also an easy and classic way to earn a little extra cash. And this is not even weeding or other forms of gardening! Offering to cut people's lawns can help you earn a little extra without too much work! (Carosa, 2021)

Becoming A Video Editor

All you need is one great video editing software and take on some good video editing gigs online. You don't have to be a movie master pro, and you can take your time building up more jobs and even possibly a career! Video editors are high in demand after all! (Kate, 2020)

Sell Your Art

If art is something you enjoy and have a talent in, then why not make some money off of it? Selling your work on Etsy or eBay as well as on private platforms is a great way to kickstart this journey (Bell, 2021).

Start A Blog

The reason why this is ideal for you at your age is that you need some time and patience to earn money here. You can earn money from a blog when you have a bigger readership. Then you can do affiliate marketing, sponsored posts, and ads. All these

are a little technical, so ask an adult for help if need be (Bell, 2021).

Now here is a list of plenty more ideas you can certainly consider:

- Taking online surveys
- Creating a YouTube Channel
- Holding a Garage Sale

- Babysit
- Photography
- Selling T-Shirts
- Sell Your Crafts
- Create Games
- Enter into Contests
- Build Websites for Other People
- Cleaning Service
- Run Errands
- Setup of Social Media Accounts
- Organize Closets
- Shoe Shining
- Carpet Cleaning
- Window Washing
- Selling Gold Balls - collecting them on golf courses that had been lost. Clean them and resell

***Take note:**

There are other job opportunities such as pet sitting or dog walking, but the reason why this was not mentioned is because of the danger posed when dealing with other people's animals. Although the majority of animals are well trained. Depending on your age and your experience it is best to take on jobs with animals if you are confident, secure, and have a greater understanding of how to deal with difficult pets. Again, many of these jobs listed have their risks, but with pets, it can be unpredictable. Be sure that your parents are aware of each job you want to take on. If they can get involved and help you out it would be even better!

As you can see, there are plenty of jobs available for anyone who has the work ethic and set their minds to it! You can do it!

Chapter 4: Banking

Where do people normally store their money? Well, if you answered a bank. That would be correct. After all, money is safer behind a vault and security guards than under a pillow in your house. The banks also make it easy to make payments for shopping with the use of credit cards, and even now mobile apps that simply scan and pay. To use those tools, you will need a bank account. That is why it is best to know what you can do about it.

History of Banking

So, this poses the question, where did banking start? Banks have been around for a while now, but they share important history for you to know and understand. Banking has been existing since the first currencies were truly minted. The currency was commonly in coins, created for taxation. When empires started growing, there had to be a system where people could pay and distribute wealth.

Banking began when empires needed a form or method to make payments for foreign services or goods with items that could very easily be exchanged. Coins varied in size, but eventually, they got replaced by fragile paper.

But before paper bills were designed, the coins needed safe storage space. Houses were so insecure, and coins weighed a lot. It was impractical to travel around with the money, and ancient homes  could not keep their wealth safe in vaults. In the Roman era, the wealthy people resorted to storing their goods under the basements of temples. Because the temples were filled with priests as well as temple workers, there was a natural assumption to their honesty, and that their belongings were safe (Beattie, 2021).

There are even records of Egypt, Rome, Greece, and Babylon that had temples that loan money out (Wikipedia contributors, 2021). This means people in ancient times had debts with the temples! Temples worked a little like a bank for many of the cities. This is why they were the first to be attacked when people stormed a city.

Coins were a lot easier to hoard because of their small size, and merchants even took to borrowing and repaying with interest to those who were desperately in need. Temples were the places that handled bigger loans for people, even sovereigns.

So Where Was the First Official Bank?

Would it surprise you if you knew it was in Rome? The Romans were good at building and paperwork. Most spending, loaning, and borrowing occurred at an institutional bank there. Julius Caesar had changed a law, allowing banks to take land if the people who owed money could not pay it back in time. This caused a massive shift in the power banks had over people as well as the noblemen because many of them had massive debts that they just passed on to their descendants unless of course, the lineage died out (Beattie, 2021).

However, the Roman Empire did come to an end - but many of the banking institutions survived - normally in the form of papal bankers from the Roman Empire as well as the Knights of Templar. Some people acted as small-time moneylenders. They tended to compete against the church.

Visa Royal

Many of the monarchs became aware of the power that lay within the banking institutions. The banks that existed had many loans taken out by people who ruled. This caused hard times to the treasury because the king could make extravagant purchases without much need to pay the banks back.

It had come to such a point that in 1557, King Phillip II from Spain had created so much debt in his country - that he caused the world's first national form of bankruptcy, then the second, then the third, then fourth at a rapid pace (Koenigsberger).

Modern Banking

Banking was already existing within the British Empire when a man by the name of Adam Smith worked to limit the state's power and involvement in a bank. This opened the world to capitalism-which is allowing businesses to grow and expand without the government getting involved.

At first, though, Adam's idea did not seem to help. An average bank may just have survived for five years, but Alexander Hamilton created a system that worked to keep banks afloat, he created a liquid market and pushed out the competition that was not legal (Wikipedia contributors, 2021).

Because many of the other banks had not been legal when this system was established, there was a great level of mistrust people had for them.

Merchant Banks

Many of the duties within an economy were to be handled by that of a national banking system. This meant that loans and business finance were normally controlled by merchant banks. They used their connections to build political as well as financial power.

In the year 1907, a collapse in business shares caused many people to panic. They stormed into banks trying to sell their stock. This caused a huge knock on the value of the shares of the business. J.P. Morgan took control to stop the panic and cause people to calm down (The Investopedia Team, 2021).

In 1929, the trade slowed down, and there was a stock market crash (where the value of many businesses and investments failed). It was called a Black Tuesday because many people lost their money as well as their jobs. This in turn caused a disaster for the country overall, and all banks had to face massive consequences. After this, there were very clear rules set out for banks (Wikipedia, 2021).

Banks were given rules to follow for the people to trust in them, but no one believed them, and the area remained in depression (when there are greater expenses than income flowing through a city).

However, World War II played a part in the recovery of the country and saved banks from being obliterated. The war needed billions of dollars to carry on, and many companies decided to build huge credit with them, and eventually turn into a global market. Finally, the countries started to settle. The trust between banks grew, and an average person had good access to insurance, mortgages, and other forms of credit-credit means of borrowing money (Goodwin, 2021).

Knowing about the banks, in general, isn't enough to proceed. There is much more to know and understand about the banks and how they work. Whenever you need to connect your finances with any bank, you need to have an account there. A bank account is an account that the bank maintains to save and transact your finances. Banks or other financial institutions keep the records of your financial transaction through your bank accounts (Wikipedia).

Types of Accounts

Now chances are your parents both own a bank account. You may or may not already have one yourself, but have you ever wondered why there are different account names? Well, let's take a look at the different bank accounts you can indeed open.

Current Account

This is known as a deposit account for traders, entrepreneurs, business owners, and people who need to both make as well as receive payments on a more regular basis. This means the money tends to come and go quickly, flowing to and fro (thus called liquid). There is no limit to the number of transactions you can make in a day, and you cannot earn any form of interest with this account.

Savings Account

This works like a deposit account. You place money and you earn some interest (a small amount of money gets paid into your account over a certain period). The number of transactions you can make on this account are limited and there are different kinds of savings accounts. Some offer higher interest (more payments received every month), but that normally means you need to give a greater warning when you want to withdraw money from your account. A savings account can be opened for children, women, seniors, families, and more.

Salary Account

This is an account that is connected to you, your employer, and the bank. Because you are not likely to have a job at this time, this account is not too important to know about. However, just so you know, this bank account is used to have your monthly salary paid in if you do have a job.

Fixed Deposit Account

This is where you have an account where you receive a fixed amount of interest (payment) every month or every three months. However, this does mean you need to pay a certain amount of money to open an account like this, and you have to wait before you can withdraw money.

Checking Accounts

A checking account is used to deposit the payment and keep daily spending records. This account comes with checks and a debit card. You can use these checks and cards to spend the money that is not in your account actually.

Investment and Retirement Accounts

When you need to open an account in a bank, you can ask for an investment account. This will be a brokerage account for your investments. You can use it to invest your money in bonds, mutual funds, bonds, and other financial items.

(Nova Credit, 2020)

Chapter 5: Safety While Earning

If you have worked on the internet before, you are probably familiar with viruses'. But considering that your plan is to invest online, what does that mean for you? It means that you have to take extra steps to stay safe! You may not be able to see the risks or dangers (considering they are hidden in a line of code), but you need to be aware that there are some things you need to be careful of while working online - especially when there is money involved.

Consider the internet is one big marketplace. In the marketplace, you can find all sorts of goodies and items to buy and sell. But in between, there are a couple of people trying to sell you duds or literally just steal your money from you. There are others who already

try to destroy and corrupt what you already have. There are many pickpockets, trying to steal your information and use it to either sell or get more money from you (Safe Search Kid, 2021).

This is how the internet works, and this is why you need to follow certain rules in order to avoid the bad guys on the internet. Although this does not make you completely bulletproof, you will be good at handling 90% of the worst and common criminals on the internet out there. Now isn't that just neat? This is because the people on the internet target the gullible and the people desperate to make money. They love to sweet talk people into giving their information. Don't fall for this trap!

Top Rules to Stay Safe Online

The following are the rules to implement when you decide to work online. These rules help you to stay safe from scams and online fraud.

Keep the Information You Share Limited

Personal information should be limited at least and avoided at most. Most employers and customers online do not need to know where you live, as well as altogether your bank account details (unless you are making a purchase on the website - if so, make sure it is a safe website). When it comes to your life online, do not hand out any unnecessary personal information about yourself publically either - especially on social media. There is such a thing as an online stalker, and this is where they can get most of the information from you (Safe Search Kid, 2021).

Consider this, you won't be handing out your credit card or street address or even your last name on the street. So why would you want to do that to millions of people who are online?

Keeping the Privacy Settings, You Have On

People in the marketplace want to know as much information about you as they can, but here is the problem, so do the hackers. And you can give them a backdoor where you browse and the social media that you use. But it can also be up to you to take control of your information. The people can't take what you don't upload, or if you close the backdoor with some steel bars. Try either on your own or with an adult to boost the privacy settings on all the software and apps that you use. Even Facebook has very specialized settings for you to use, making it hard for companies and hackers to actually discover your personal information.

Being A Safe browser

Google cannot filter every bad website and considering you would not normally walk in a bad neighborhood, don't browse in a bad online neighborhood. Cybercriminals love to use clickbait as well as different forms of content to lure you in. The problem is, if you click onto one bad website, you can let malware in. So, it is best to have your anti-virus set up to scan the website before even entering and be very careful of suggested links. Even if you visit a safe website, sometimes ads are placed to lead you to a bad one.

A Great Way to Play It Safe, Use a VPN

So, what on earth is a VPN? Well, let's start with an IP address. The IP Address is basically your digital signal that you give whenever you are visiting various kinds of websites, you are leaving your IP address, indicating to the websites where you are.

Now, this can be tracked, and although it is mostly harmless, you want to keep the cybercriminals away from you. This is where VPN comes in. VPN hides your IP Address and keeps you from being tracked or traced. This makes using the websites infinitely safer, and this is especially important at your age.

Be Very Careful of What You Download

The main goal of bad people on the internet is tricking you into downloading something onto your computer. Normally this gives easy and direct access for viruses and malware to infect your computer to either steal or corrupt information. It may all look well and innocent, but if you are not 100% completely sure what you are downloading is safe then you need to take a step back and reconsider what you are doing.

Choose Strong Passwords

It is easy to choose passwords that you can remember, but they tend to be easy as well as weak. It is up to you to choose strong passwords, despite it taking longer and being tougher to remember. Strong passwords keep people from breaking in easily. In fact, it can prevent many hackers from attempting to get inside.

Keep the Antivirus Up to Date

New viruses are constantly being made, and this is why you need to constantly keep your antivirus up to date. This is because antivirus is doing its best to keep up, combating viruses and identifying malware to keep your computers safe. Therefore the best plan of action is to keep it updated.

So, these steps are all good and well, but what do you do to avoid possible investment scams? This is where you have to filter through the different investment choices and be able to choose from the options. There is always the risk of choosing the wrong one and losing your money. There are certain steps you can take (Safe Search Kid, 2021).

Avoiding Investment Scams

First, don't be scared to ask questions. Most con artists say that you won't investigate before you give the money. However, do not just ask the questions to them, find out information from other sources, and take your time to do more forms of your own research. People are very verbal on the web, and the likelihood that you are the first one

to be scammed is very small. So it is very easy to discover scams if you just ask the right questions.

Any investments you need to make are worthy of a decent amount of research. Looking into different financial statements or having an adult look into it is always a good idea. The less information you can find about a company, the more suspicious it can truly become (Fowler, 2021).

Know your salesperson - you need to spend some time getting to know the person offering the investments. Even if you have known them a little while beforehand, you want to make sure they are actually licensed to sell the specific securities in the states, and you can even check the disciplinary history of brokers and advisers completely free on the FINRA's and SEC's databases. (These are databases making sure all the public information is readily available for everyone to get access to.)

Be very careful of offers that were not solicited (basically they approached you - you did not approach them). Even if they have been praised online but do not offer the proper financial information from different/dependant sources. This could be something known as the "pump and dump" scheme, where something is bound to go wrong, and it is near impossible to track your money down.

Familiarize yourself and your family members with all the various kinds of fraud that come with investments. The more you know about the different types of frauds, the more easily you'll be able to spot them when they come your way.

Be careful as well of the following persuasion tactics commonly used to convince you into making the wrong investment:

- ***If it sounds way too good to be true, then it is.*** This is because riches are promised for investments that do not provide enough information on how it will go. Besides, all investments have risks. To promise otherwise is plain foolish or it is a scam. People take the risk away to help people invest - when in reality, investing in someone or business that makes promises such as these are the biggest risks after all.

- ***Guaranteed returns are not a thing*** - but scammers and con artists love to make such promises. As mentioned above, each investment has too much risk. If they try to plant images in your head of someone who is rich, be very careful. They like to play on the desperate.

- ***Everyone is busy buying it*** - again, another massive scam. This is because they try to create FOMO (fear of missing out). However, if you tackle that statement you will find it crumbling to the ground. This is just a tactic used to get people to invest as quickly as possible.

- ***Reciprocity*** - fraudsters even do their best to lure people in by inviting them to free seminars or webinars. It works for them doing a small favor for you, in return, you can do a massive favor for them. So always make sure you know that the product is right for you, understand exactly what you are buying as well as any and all associated fees that actually come with this.

(*Investment Fraud Attorneys*, n.d.)

Verifying

The best step to root out fraudsters is by verifying the information that is sent to you. For example, the most basic method is by going directly to the source and calling people. Especially when it comes to news about people and more that is posted on social media.

Second, it is always best to rely on first-hand witnesses. So, if you can discover anybody who has invested in a certain product or business - it would be ideal to have a conversation with them first if at all possible.

When checking things out on social media, check out the credibility of a person. Be very careful of brand-new accounts. This is because many scammers are rooted out quickly, their accounts blocked, and therefore are in constant need to make new accounts. Check out a person's friends and followers, is the account used on a regular basis?

When you are verifying website information, you can check with WHOIS lookup, in order to check who really registered the URL. This will allow you to access the internet archive and get a good idea of the person and whether or not the information they give is credible (*Common Scams and Frauds | USAGov*, n.d.).

Next, you can even verify images, such as checking out the language, license plates, signs, languages, etc. You can also check out TinEye which allows you to see where an image had actually come from - basically, whether it was copy-pasted (a good tactic also to discover whether or not you are being catfished).

And there you have it! Caution to stay safe while investing, tactics to verify the information, and general ideas on how to avoid getting scammed. When you are learning how to earn and invest, you must learn about budgeting and how to manage your income. If you follow most of these steps, you are already one step ahead of the average investor. And you are still so young!

Chapter 6: Budgeting - Learn How to Handle Your Income

So what happens when you start earning money? What do you do then? Well, there is a very important step to learn in the world of finances and investing. And do you want to know a big secret? Most people don't practice this step as they should. As a matter of fact, many of them don't even know how to do this! Do you have a guess?

If you said backflips. You are correct, but there is also budgeting. What on earth is budgeting? It is basically a plan you set up with your money to make sure you spend and save the right amounts. Most people do not budget as they should.

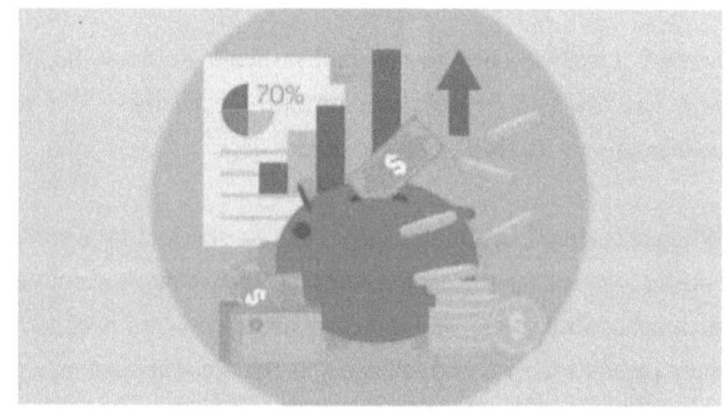

If you learn the secrets of budgeting at a young age, you will be doing yourself a massive favor. This is because this well-crafted skill will keep your money in check, allowing you to make sure you don't overspend on any items, and the money actually goes where it needs to go. So here are some steps on how to budget properly - and the faster you learn this, the better! (Bruce, 2021)

Basics of Budgeting

Now remember the following, budgeting is actually a living thing. This is because it is constantly moving, having expenses, income, and everything to keep track of. Your budget will also always be changing as your life changes. Expecting it to remain exactly the same is basically saying nothing will be changing in your life either. But you already know that what happened at the beginning of this year and what will be happening at the end is very different. So here is a step-by-step guide of what you need to do to set up a budget.

Note the amount of income coming in

First, start off by making an estimate of the amount of money you have coming in on a monthly or weekly basis. Rather underestimate than overestimate, and make sure you write this number down.

Track the spending that you do

Keep track of any purchases you are making. If you don't know how much you are spending, how can you possibly plan and keep track of it in the long haul? It would also be a lot easier to see where you are overspending, and where you can actually start cutting costs.

Set The Goals

Want to save up for an Xbox game? Or do you want to buy a camera? Set goals! How much money you want to earn, how much money you want to spend, and how much money you want to save. Goals can help you form a plan which is the next step.

Making a Plan

With all the expenses and income, you have tracked, now it is time to set up a plan for the following few months. Write down how much you should make as well as how much you are going to spend - break your expenses down into different categories. Even your savings will count in this budget, as you want to make sure every penny you have is spoken for.

Adjustments

Once you have tried out your first budget, you will come to pick up on any changes that may need to be made. Spent too much on popcorn? Cut the costs and place the money over into savings for the car. Skip a movie night in order to make sure you can spend money for your outing with your friends the next day. All these will help you pick and choose - a very important skill to learn when it comes to budgeting, life, and finances in general.

Never Stop Checking in

Make sure you are always keeping proper track of your finances. Make sure you know that you are staying on par and learn to adjust if you happen to overspend. At the end of the day, you want to learn the habit of keeping track of your expenses and sticking to the plan. This is by far the biggest favor you can truly do for yourself as you start growing up and have to face the financial predicaments later in life.

But this may beg the question, why is budgeting so important? Why is it necessary to help your financial journey? Well, here are a few good reasons why you need to budget (Schwab Brokerage).

Why Should You Budget?

Firstly, the budget will really help you to get good control of your finances. Just because you earn money does not mean you actually have control of it. You will find your older self, thanking you left right and center for mastering this skill. Just because it really can hinder or destroy your success if you do not know this skill.

Secondly, being able to budget allows you to achieve any goals you may have. Whether it is your college funds or your vacation, or your latest cell phone. Being able to budget allows you to set money aside for things that you want even though they may be more expensive. All you need is the proper time and patience for it (Khan, 2017).

Thirdly, budgeting will really help to keep you honest. If you keep a good track record of your money and what you are spending it on, it can keep you accountable to reach your goals. If you keep a good budget, then you have to keep track of every single coin you spent on. This is a good, as well as a powerful motivator to keep your spending on track, allowing you to reach your goals faster.

Budgeting can also help improve bad habits or reduce the chances of you getting one. If you learn how to budget at a very early age, then you are doing yourself a massive favor. This is because you will not learn many bad habits that people who do not budget learn. It teaches you self-control, a very important trait to be successful in everyday life (Schwab Brokerage).

Finally, budgeting can really help you to avoid debt or help you get rid of debt as quickly as possible. It is never nice to owe someone money, so good budgeting can help you avoid it or help you get rid of it so much quicker. Now is that not neat?

So, in the world of budgeting, you have now seen the steps you can take and why you should take it. Especially at your age, there is not a lot to keep track of, so it puts you a step ahead. Budgeting will be easier, and by the time it starts to get more complicated, you will have such a good habit of when to spend and when to save that it can hardly be called a challenge.

Chapter 7: When to Spend and When to Save

In line with budgeting, you may be good at planning, but how can you stick to the plan? This is by learning the balance of spending and saving. This can be a tough and tricky habit to adopt, and I am here to help! Just like learning how to mine, you need a few tricks in order to find the golden nugget faster.

The Art of Self-Control

Why does self-control really matter? Well, it is a form of willpower, it is having the ability to control yourself, your actions, and even your thoughts in order to get a better outcome. How many times do you remember people getting angry at you, and things just get worse from there on? This is because the person lacked the self-control necessary in order to really practice patience despite getting really mad. This is self-control, and it is a very **important aspect of people's lives.**

Self-control can also help you to eliminate distractions, do better at school, and even get to your chores. It means you are less inclined to get in trouble and do better. And when it comes to budgeting, it makes life a whole lot easier. If you are trying to invest, and work on earning money, then the need for self-control is equally critical (Team Understood, 2021).

So here are a couple of steps you can learn to practice a little more self-control. Consider adding it to your everyday life, surprise your friends and family members!

Out of Sight - Out of Mind

When it comes to anything that can distract you during your work and school and finances, keep it out of sight! If your phone keeps you away from your budgeting, ask your mother to keep it for you until you are done with your budgeting (present the proof). If you have the habit of playing video games right after school, pack it away and only bring it out once you have completed all your homework. Little tips like that can truly make all the difference in the world (*Thinking Skills: Focus*, 2017).

Reward Yourself for Work Accomplished

Why not buy yourself a bag of candy to reward yourself whenever you get something done? Or it is even better if your parents can set up a system for you. Treat yourself to a chocolate or a toy whenever you get a certain amount of money, or to a candy whenever you clean your room (Good Character, 2020).

Set Yourself Reminders

The best way to get something done is to remind yourself to do it. Set up on your phone or calendar all the tasks you need to get done and remember to do it! It is very easy to lose track of all the matters and items in life. But with a daily if not an hourly reminder, you can get everything you need done.

Allow Yourself to Take a Break

Teatime breaks, lunchtime breaks, and even afternoon breaks are all needed. Allow yourself time to play, have fun, go out with friends, and still experience parts of your childhood. You are allowed to have your fun. You are allowed to take a break. If not, life can become dull and dreary. This is why many adults themselves can become incredibly bored of their work. It is because they do not have any room to have a little bit of fun and joy in their life.

Turn the Tasks of "Must Do" into a "Want To"

This is where you need to decide that you want to do your tasks instead of needing to. It is a mindset that you need to adopt. For example, instead of thinking, I must do the dishes - you should say I want to do the dishes. It may seem too simple or too easy. But sometimes the too simple and too easy solutions are what gets the tasks done after all.

Practice Planning

Take each and every day as a new opportunity to practice your ability to plan and stick to it. This means that each day you can work on practicing your self-control. After all, if you are familiar with sports or drawing, you will have to practice each and every day. The same can be said for planning. In order to get better at planning, you need practice after all (Sippl, 2021).

Finally, when you think you have learned a lot about money, how to earn and spend it, it is time to jump into the field of investing. Get your parents or adults involved in your decisions. When you decide to invest, let them help you stay on track and keep focused. After all, they can keep you accountable, and help practice your planning, budgeting, and spending. It may seem dreadful at first, but in reality, it would be very helpful throughout the investing process.

Chapter 8: Investing Money

Investing is one of the wisest, most productive methods at earning money. This is known as a passive form of income. What does it mean to be passive? Well, very little work is put into it, but you will still receive money! Now, this may seem a little too good to be true. Well, it can be - if you are not careful. This is why it is time to take a peek at investments to understand everything you need to know. For example, when starting with an investment, a lot of work needs to be done before being able to just let the money grow.

Introduction To Investing

Investing is always changing. That is why it is best to jump on the bus as early as possible and learn to stay up to date. But there are a couple of basic principles that once you undertake them, you should have a foundational knowledge of investing. As there are some core principles which can help you succeed in earning money, even at your age!

Investing is placing money into a business, asset, or another potential item in hopes of getting a return (profit from the money that was initially placed).

First, investments are made of a risk ladder. This means, depending on where you are in investing, there are higher risks and lower risks. What are the risks I am referring to? Well, sometimes you spend money, but then you do not get anything in return. Some investments have a bigger chance of you losing money in comparison to others (Picardo, 2021).

But here is one big rule in investing: there can never be a 100% guarantee of making a profit. If anyone tells you that an investment will always pay off, be very careful. No true investment works this way, and you may be falling into a scam.

Different Types of Investment

Now, the simplest and safest investment form is a cash bank deposit. They are by far the easiest, simplest forms of investing and safest too. Because you will have a greater understanding of what you will be receiving.

However, this form of investing does not normally beat inflation. *What is inflation?* Have you ever realized how items become more expensive as time passes by? Well, this is inflation, and the value of $100 gradually becomes less and less as time passes by. So to 'keep' the value of the $100, you will have to earn the same amount of money as inflation rises. But when it comes to cash bank deposits, you do not normally earn enough - which means you might still be losing money.

Bonds

Bonds are a form of debt that is created between the investor and the person who is borrowing. You will be lending out money to someone, and they will be paying you back over time with interest. Naturally, the interest you receive will be the profit of your investment. You can normally buy bonds from corporations or a government agency and is a very common form of financing for businesses.

The amount of interest you earn depends on the interest rate (percentage) and so people tend to invest in bonds when interest rates happen to be rising in banks etc.

How can I make money with this? While you are busy lending the money, the person borrowing it will be paying interest. Depending on how old the bond is and when the money is returned, depends on how much money you make. Naturally the longer the money is borrowed, the more interest, and therefore more profit (Dragon, 2021).

Stocks

This is likely to be the kind of investing that you will be focusing on for now. Stocks are small parts of ownership for a business. The business then pays you with their profits for owning a part of their business. This is normally called a dividend. The amount of dividend you get depends on the number of stocks you have as well as how much profit the business has made. The harsh truth is that if the business struggles to make money for a certain period, then you are not likely to receive a dividend. So you have to be very careful with the business you happen to choose.

How can I make money here? Well, you will buy stock (normally with the help of an adult) - remember to do some research on the business first. Ask yourself - is the business doing well? How old is it? What are people saying about this business? The older, more established the business is with a history of making a profit, the better. Once you have purchased stocks, you can either wait for the value of the stock to rise and resell it. Then you make money from the extra cash you have received, or you can wait and receive dividends. Tip: if you see the value of the stock sinking over a certain period, it is best to sell your stock to make sure you do not have a big loss (Adams, 2021).

Mutual Funds

This is when you place money into one singular fund. But this fund happens to buy up a variety of different stocks. Then split up the dividends and share this with you. You can either manage this yourself or have others manage it for you. The advantage of this is that you spread your risk. It means that if one business were to fail, you can still make a profit from the other profits that are succeeding (Thune, 2021).

How can I make money?

Buy into the fund from a managing firm or discount brokerage. It would be recommended to consider a managing firm at this point as you are still building up experience. Oftentimes with discount brokerages, you need to tell them what to buy whereas the firms buy into companies based on their experiences and knowledge. Take a look at what businesses they invest in and learn why they made those decisions. You can learn a lot while making money. Which is a bonus!

Commodities

This is a pirate's treasure, where you buy gold, silver, or any number of items in this world that are valuable. Then you wait for the best value of the silver or gold which you have purchased and resell it for a profit (*What Are Commodity Funds?*, n.d.).

Now there are many other options for investing, but at this point and time, you are not likely to be able to afford these kinds of investing:

- *Real estate investing* - this is when you purchase a house and rent it out
- *Hedge funds and private equity funds* - this is when you invest in a large variety of assets which can cost up to $1 million or even higher and can take a long time before you can receive the money again
- *Cryptocurrencies* - this has a lot of potential in making money, but without experience and an in-depth understanding of how crypto works, you can get yourself into big trouble. It is too high of a risk to consider as a good form of investment. People have to invest in this at their own risk and is not recommended here - especially at your age (James Royal, Ph.D., 2021).

Top Tips when Making An Investment

You can't always walk into a building and tell the people there you want to invest. And depending on your age, you may also not necessarily be at the right age. This is where your parents or a grown adult can help you. Once you have made enough money and you want to start investing, you will need to complete a couple of steps:

1. *Choose where you are going to invest* - you want to know where you are going to invest - such as bonds, or banks, or mutual funds. Once you understand that you can move on to the next step (Coombes, 2021).

2. *Do your research.* You want to know everything you can about the businesses you are interested in. If you struggle to understand what is going on, ask an adult, if they even struggle, don't consider investing in that business.

3. *Get more information* - The less information you can find out about the area you want to invest in, the riskier the investment. Preferably you want to invest in a completely transparent organization - most information is easy to get a hold of then (Coombes, 2021).

4. *Find a good broker* - brokers are people who normally purchase the shares for you. You can either get a full-service broker, but they will be more expensive and more inclined for people who are investing full time (they do help to build a financial plan as well as keep you informed on the most potential investments), or you can get a discount broker. Then, you or your parents will tell them what to do, buy and sell in return for a small commission fee (familyeducation.com, 2017).

5. *Invest!* When you have found a trustworthy broker, it is time to invest.

6. *Wait and keep an eye on it.* If you see things are going well, leave the investment there, but if you see that the value of the investment is reducing, try to cut costs by selling it as soon as possible. However, ask for advice on this matter. Because some investments may sink in value only to bounce back and make a profit later.

There you have it! This is how you can start placing your money and watching it grow! Suddenly it does not seem so hard or complicated after all. However, it is again recommended to have an adult help you with these decisions because many of them have a better experience. However, remember to do your research, and that the decision should ultimately be in your hands.

Leave a 1-click review!

I would be incredibly grateful if you take just 60 seconds to write just a brief review on Amazon, even if it's just a few sentences.

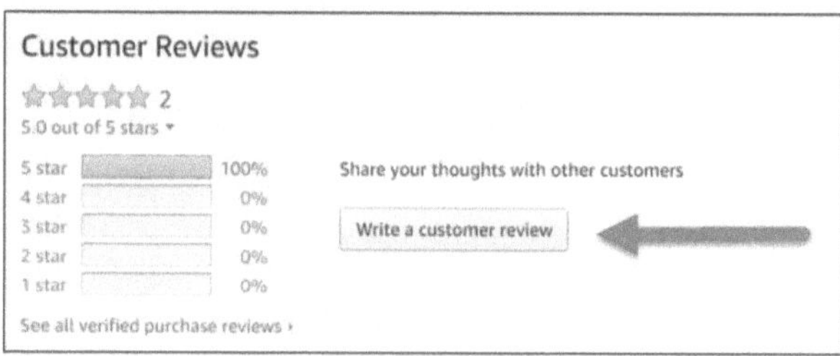

https://www.amazon.com/review/create-review-asin=B09ML9VJCF

Conclusion

Here we are at the end of our tale. You have now mined for some golden nuggets, and you have the information to do so! Be patient and kind with yourself, as it will not be an easy journey. It never is with investing, but it doesn't mean it can't be fun!

Remember, the primary responsibility of the breadwinner is to the parents and adults in your life. What you want to do now is learn how to earn money without having to rush into it like grown-ups do. This is the fun part of being a child, is using your time to earn a little extra money without all the necessary stresses and more!

Furthermore, any help you may need or have should be left to an adult. Struggling to open a bank account? Have an adult help you! Want someone to keep you responsible for all the budgeting and checking on your investments? Adults can help you too! Now it may seem quite dreary from time to time, but in reality, making money is very rewarding -opening doors in which you can indeed participate in either buying fun stuff or actually going on an adventure! Furthermore, there is nothing quite so satisfying as learning skills that most adults don't even practice! This will make you far wiser than the average person!

Also remember, planning is key, without a good plan, how on earth are you supposed to move forward? But a good plan only comes with practice and making sure you stick with the plan can yet again come with repetition. Make plans and learn how to stick to them every single day. Soon you won't be running late for anything, your homework will be on par, and you still should have free time to enjoy yourself as well as make some money. After all, your schedule should not be close to adults.

Remember, finally, to have fun but also to stay safe! The internet is crowded with bad people, so you have to be smart about your approach, otherwise again it can get you into trouble. Make sure whatever computer that you use has the anti-virus and proper equipment to keep your information safe. After all, you don't want anyone stealing your

hard work.

And finally, we reach the end of the mine. It has been a long day, but certainly worth it! Don't be afraid to go back and review where necessary. After all, it is quite easy to forget stuff and facts much like the dates in the history lesson. If you are good with remembering those, then well done! Because most people are terrible with dates.

And thus, we now have to bid farewell. It has been such an amazing journey to walk with you, teaching all kinds of wonderful and practical matters in investing. I hope you have learned a lot and see you in the world of finances!

Reviews are a great way for both adults and kids alike to discover new books to read in the future. So, if you enjoyed this book and would recommend it to others, please leave a review on Amazon! Talk about your favorite element of the book and who would enjoy reading it.

Thank you!

My other books you will love!

Amazon.com/dp/B09ML95Q6N

Amazon.com/dp/B09ML9VJCF

Don't forget to grab your GIFT!!!

http://daphnemcooper.com/parenting.pdf

Joining the PME Community

Looking to meet other parents that can help you on your parenting journey? If so, then check out the Parenting Made Easy (PME) Community here:

https://www.facebook.com/groups/293830159257919/

References

A.K. (2021, January 15). *Benefits of Being Financially Stable*. Child Abuse Prevention, Treatment & Welfare Services | Children's Bureau. Retrieved November 10, 2021, from https://www.all4kids.org/news/blog/benefits-of-being-financially-stable/

Adams, R. C. (2021, October 17). *12 Stocks for Kids: Kid-Friendly Stocks to Begin Investing [2021]*. Young and the Invested. Retrieved November 13, 2021, from https://youngandtheinvested.com/stocks-for-kids/

Anderson, K. (2021, April 1). *Guide to the Barter Economy & the Barter System History*. MintLife Blog. https://mint.intuit.com/blog/personal-finance/guide-to-the-barter-economy-the-barter-system-history/

Bank Panic of 1907 Definition. (2021, September 28). Investopedia. Retrieved November 10, 2021, from https://www.investopedia.com/terms/b/bank-panic-of-1907.asp

(Barnum, Forbes). https://www.forbes.com/quotes/7311/

Beattie, A. B. (2021, August 23). *The History of Money: From Barter to Banknotes*. Investopedia. Retrieved November 11, 2021, from https://www.investopedia.com/articles/07/roots_of_money.asp

Beattie, A. B. (2021, May 29). *The Evolution of Banking Over Time*. Investopedia. Retrieved November 11, 2021, from https://www.investopedia.com/articles/07/banking.asp

Bell, S. B. (2021, August 13). *How to Make Money as a Kid*. Money under 30. Retrieved November 10, 2021, from https://www.moneyunder30.com/how-to-make-money-as-a-kid

Blessing, E. B. (2020, December 16). *The Coinage Act of 1792*. Investopedia. Retrieved November 12, 2021, from https://www.investopedia.com/terms/c/the-coinage-act-of-1972.asp

Booth, B. (2020, January 31). *It's not just about saving. Teach your teen to invest now to set them up for a financially healthy life*. CNBC. Retrieved

November 10, 2021, from https://www.cnbc.com/2020/01/29/teaching-teenagers-to-invest-now-will-set-them-up-for-life.html

Bruce, K. (2021, May 14). *Budgeting for Kids: How to Teach Budgeting From Age 3 to 18*. Freedom Sprout.Retrieved November 12, 2021, from https://freedomsprout.com/budgeting-for-kids/

Budgeting. (n.d.). Schwab Brokerage. Retrieved November 12, 2021, from https://www.schwabmoneywise.com/teaching-kids/budgeting

Carosa, C. (2021, July 26). *Yes, Babysitting And Lawn Mowing Money Can Go Into A Child IRA*. Forbes. Retrieved November 8, 2021, from https://www.forbes.com/sites/chriscarosa/2021/07/25/yes-babysitting-and-lawn-mowing-money-can-go-into-a-child-ira/

Carlson, B. (2021, October 6). *An Unhealthy Obsession with Money*. Https://Awealthofcommonsense.Com/2021/10/an-Unhealthy-Obsession-with-Money/. Retrieved November 8, 2021, from https://awealthofcommonsense.com/2021/10/an-unhealthy-obsession-with-money/

Charge It. (2017, August 7). National Museum of American History. Retrieved November 11, 2021, from https://americanhistory.si.edu/american-enterprise-exhibition/consumer-era/charge-it

Common Scams and Frauds | USAGov. (n.d.). USA Government. Retrieved November 12, 2021, from https://www.usa.gov/common-scams-frauds

Coombes, A. (2021, February 10). *What to Invest In: Choosing Your Investments*. NerdWallet. Retrieved November 13, 2021, from https://www.nerdwallet.com/article/investing/what-to-invest-in

Corporate Finance Institute. (2021, February 2). *Bartering*. Retrieved November 7, 2021, from https://corporatefinanceinstitute.com/resources/knowledge/economics/bartering/

DeNicola, L. D. N. (2020, July 9). *A guide to the different types of bank accounts in the United States*. Nova Credit. Retrieved November 10, 2021, from https://www.novacredit.com/resources/a-guide-to-the-different-types-of-bank-accounts-in-the-united-states/

Dragon, D. (2021, September 11). *What Bonds Should You Buy for Your Kids?* MyBankTracker. Retrieved November 13, 2021, from https://www.mybanktracker.com/savings/faq/buying-savings-bonds-kids-115764

Dunn, E., & Courtney, C. C. (2021, October 11). *Does More Money Really Make Us More Happy?* Harvard Business Review. Retrieved November 7, 2021, from https://hbr.org/2020/09/does-more-money-really-makes-us-more-happy

Familyeducation.com. (2017, August 2). *Online Trading for Kids.* FamilyEducation. Retrieved November 13, 2021, from https://www.familyeducation.com/life/earning-money/online-trading-kids

Fowler, J. F. (2021, October 27). *10 Common Scams Targeted at Teens.* Investopedia. Retrieved November 11, 2021, from https://www.investopedia.com/financial-edge/1012/common-scams-targeted-at-teens.aspx

Goodwin, D. (2021, April 9). *The Way We Won: America's Economic Breakthrough During World War II.* The American Prospect. Retrieved November 12, 2021, from https://prospect.org/health/way-won-america-s-economic-breakthrough-world-war-ii/

Hayes, A. (2021, May 29). *Affluenza Definition.* Investopedia. Retrieved November 9, 2021, from https://www.investopedia.com/terms/a/affluenza.asp

Helpguidewp, Robinson, L., & Smith, M. S. (2021, July 15). *Coping with Financial Stress.* HelpGuide.Org. Retrieved November 7, 2021, from https://www.helpguide.org/articles/stress/coping-with-financial-stress.htm

History and Legacy. (n.d.). Diners Club International. Retrieved November 10, 2021, from https://www.dinersclub.com/about-us/history/

Honick, L. (2021, October 15). *The History of Currency From Bartering to the Credit Card*. Host Merchant Services. Retrieved November 10, 2021, from https://www.hostmerchantservices.com/articles/the-history-of-currency-from-bartering-to-the-credit-card/

How to become a child influencer on Instagram featuring Lovemalaha. (2019, November 19). KULTKID. Retrieved November 10, 2021, from https://kultkid.com/blogs/blog/how-to-become-a-child-influencer-on-instagram

Investment Fraud Attorneys. (n.d.). Meyer Wilson. Retrieved November 11, 2021, from https://www.investorclaims.com/library/5-common-persuasion-tactics-used-by-investment-s/

Investopedia, & Beattie, A. B. (2011, November 4). *The Evolution Of Banking*. Forbes. Retrieved November 11, 2021, from https://www.forbes.com/sites/investopedia/2011/11/03/the-evolution-of-banking/?sh=5f6b7bee6987

James Royal, Ph.D. (2021, November 12). *What Is Cryptocurrency? Here's What You Should Know*. NerdWallet. Retrieved November 13, 2021, from https://www.nerdwallet.com/article/investing/cryptocurrency-7-things-to-know

Kate, G. P. (2020, April 16). *How to Make Up to a Full-Time Income as a Video Editor*. Best of Budgets. Retrieved November 10, 2021, from https://www.bestofbudgets.com/full-time-income-as-a-video-editor/

Khan, S. (2017, December 26). *Making Children Learn The Benefits Of Budgeting From An Early Age*. Thrive Global. Retrieved November 12, 2021, from https://thriveglobal.com/stories/making-children-learn-the-benefits-of-budgeting-from-an-early-age/

Koenigsberger, H. Georg (n.d). Philip II. Encyclopedia Britannica. Retrieved November 11, 2021, from https://www.britannica.com/biography/Philip-II-king-of-Spain-and-Portugal

Nationwide, N. F. (2021, February 23). *How to Sell at a Farmers Market.* Now from Nationwide ®. Retrieved November 10, 2021, from https://blog.nationwide.com/how-to-sell-at-farmers-markets/

NOVA Online | Secrets of Making Money | The History of Money | PBS. (n.d.). Https://Www.Pbs.Org/Wgbh/Nova/Moolah/History.Html. Retrieved November 10, 2021, from https://www.pbs.org/wgbh/nova/moolah/history.html

Philosopher's Library. (n.d.). *Chinese Miniature Replicas - Around 1100 B.C.* Deepstash. Retrieved November 11, 2021, from https://deepstash.com/idea/106624/chinese-miniature-replicas-around-1100-bc

Philosopher's Library. (n.d.). Paypal and Digital Money - Around 1990. Deepstash. Retrieved November 11, 2021, from https://deepstash.com/idea/106632/paypal-and-digital-money-around-1990

Picardo, E. P. (2019, August 23). *What Is A Currency War And How Does It Work?* Investopedia. Retrieved November 12, 2021, from https://www.investopedia.com/articles/forex/042015/what-currency-war-how-does-it-work.asp

Picardo, E. P. (2021, May 1). *What Is Investing?* Investopedia. Retrieved November 13, 2021, from https://www.investopedia.com/terms/i/investing.asp

Santi, J. (2017, August 4). *The Secret to Happiness Is Helping Others.* TIME.Com. Retrieved November 8, 2021, from https://time.com/collection-post/4070299/secret-to-happiness/

Sippl, A. (2021, April 12). *10 Planning Skills Every Child Should Learn.* Life Skills Advocate. Retrieved November 13, 2021, from https://lifeskillsadvocate.com/blog/10-planning-skills-every-child-should-learn/

S.S.K. (2021, February 21). *Beware of Online Scams (Phishing, SMishing, Vishing).* Kid Safe. Retrieved November 13, 2021, from https://www.safesearchkids.com/protecting-against-online-scams-phishing-smishing-vishing/

Team, U. (2021, May 24). *What is self-control? Understood.Org. Retrieved November 12, 2021, from* https://www.understood.org/articles/en/self-control-what-it-means-for-kids

Teaching Guide: Appreciating Yourself - Good Character. (2020, January 17). Character Education - Social Emotional Learning - Life Skills - Lesson Plans & Curriculum. Retrieved November 11, 2021, from https://www.goodcharacter.com/elementaryschool/appreciating-yourself/

Thinking Skills: Focus. (2017, October 31). LearningWorks for Kids. Retrieved November 13, 2021, from https://learningworksforkids.com/educators/focus/

Thune, K. T. (2021, August 6). Investing Tips to Get Kids Started With Mutual Funds. The Balance. Retrieved November 12, 2021, from https://www.thebalance.com/best-mutual-funds-for-kids-2466347

What are commodity funds? (n.d.). BlackRock. Retrieved November 13, 2021, from https://www.blackrock.com/us/individual/education/commodity-funds

Wikipedia contributors. (2021, November 8). *United States Bullion Depository*. Wikipedia. Retrieved November 12, 2021, from https://en.wikipedia.org/wiki/United_States_Bullion_Depository

Wikipedia contributors. (2021, November 11). *History of banking*. Wikipedia. Retrieved November 13, 2021, from https://en.wikipedia.org/wiki/History_of_banking

Wikipedia contributors. (2021, October 24). *Wall Street Crash of 1929*. Wikipedia. Retrieved November 12, 2021, from https://en.wikipedia.org/wiki/Wall_Street_Crash_of_1929

Wikipedia contributors. (2021, August 20). *History of capitalist theory*. Wikipedia. Retrieved November 10, 2021, from https://en.wikipedia.org/wiki/History_of_capitalist_theory

Zig Ziglar Quotes. (n.d.). BrainyQuote.com. Retrieved November 13, 2021, from BrainyQuote.com Web site:

https://www.brainyquote.com/quotes/zig_ziglar_617790

Gardening For kids

Learn Gardening basics, Grow, Harvest, and Enjoy your Gardening

By Daphne M Cooper

Just for You

A free gift to our readers

http://daphnemcooper.com/parenting.pdf

Joining the PME Community

Looking to meet other parents that can help you on your parenting journey? If so, then check out the Parenting Made Easy (PME) Community here:

https://www.facebook.com/groups/293830159257919/

Introduction

Have you ever wondered how food gets from the farm to your plate? Have you ever seen a baby plant grow into a big fat strawberry? Kids who garden get to watch their food grow from seeds into something delicious. They explore the smells and colors of flowers, trees, and vegetables.

They get to touch them!

It's a chance to walk barefoot, dig in the dirt, and play with worms. A great way to keep active and stay healthy too. I wrote this book to give you a chance to experience this feeling for yourself. I am sure every day someone tells you not to watch TV or not to play your video games so much. But often nobody tells you what else you can do.

Well, I am here to change that. Today I am going to tell you about an enjoyable and rewarding activity that you can do.

You guessed it right; I am talking about gardening!

So, What is gardening?

Gardening is the process of growing plants for your own benefit or enjoyment. It can be anything from a tiny herb garden in your patio to massive fields used to produce crops. You might think it's an adults-only hobby. But it is not only for them. Everyone can do gardening, young or old, and you don't need any experience to start either!

You may need adult supervision, but I am sure by the end of reading this book, you're going to surprise everyone with your skills and knowledge.

My experience with gardening.

My love for gardening started from an early age. Over time, I experienced that gardening can be a lot of fun and an excellent way to spend your time. It is excellent for the environment because you improve your surroundings, and it helps out local wildlife too.

Watching leaves grow into bigger plants was a part of my joy as a kid and I always kept my love for gardening alive. So, when I became a mother, I found the perfect way to pass it on. After all, what can be more fun than playing in the mud and learning about the magic of nature!

Once you get fresh, healthy food that you picked yourself, you won't be able to resist it. My kids also experienced that joy, and now they are my partners in our garden.

That's why I wrote this book, to give you a secret gateway for having a common hobby with adults around you.

What to expect from this book?

From the fundamental knowledge about gardening basics to planting gardens and harvesting, you will learn it all very fast! Of course, I am not just talking about fun facts here; I am also including all the practical bits you need to know before buying tools and planting seeds.

Even if you don't like the outside or have no outside space, you can always start a small garden on your balcony or on your windowsill. Whatever fits your needs, I will give you all the tips and tricks.

But before that, you might want to know, why is gardening a good hobby for you?

Gardening is a fun activity that allows you to get in touch with nature and enjoy the greenery. It also teaches you responsibility since you will have to water your plants every day and make sure all the pests are gone before harvesting. It can be a great way of gaining experience in working with tools, and your family will enjoy it too.

But most importantly, gardening is a fun activity that can turn you into a proud gardener who always has fresh vegetables to share with friends and family. The only thing you need to do is start!

You can do it by yourself or with friends to have fun while learning something new. The greatest part is that everyone will be pleased with what you're doing since you're assisting Mother Nature!

This is one of the most important reasons gardening is popular among humans since it benefits the environment.

Impacts of Gardening

Gardening is a great activity for the planet since it involves producing food while using sustainable ways. So basically, you're growing your own little ecosystem in a pot.

What's more, your garden will attract all sorts of wildlife that can help with pest control and pollination. Expect a lot of butterflies and birds around your homegrown flowers and plants. While gardening is a great hobby on its own, it improves the overall conditions for life around you!

And last but not least, gardening is a great way to increase self-esteem and help with stress relief. After all, you can't be stressed if you're busy taking care of your garden every day.

As you spend more and more time in your garden, you will get better at it.

You will know what to do and when to do it because you are the one who has full control over this small ecosystem. It may sound funny that something so simple can have such a deep impact on your mood but hear me out.

It might start as leisure, but soon enough, it will turn into a way of life for you. Once you start taking care of your own little garden, you will be in full control of all the factors affecting it.

Of course, you can't control the weather so much, but you'll learn what plants grow better in which conditions and why.

You also won't have to worry about your plants getting eaten up by bugs; instead, you will get used to checking for pests and treating them all yourself. All of the tasks you will be doing in your gardens, such as digging and pruning, are great for your body. They increase blood circulation and make your hands stronger. All that, while being an amazing experience!

Your friends will be amazed by how much you know about gardening and will want to learn more too. You could start your own gardening club or even consider cultivating certain plants for them.

All you have to do is become a neighborhood gardening expert!

Everyone will appreciate your knowledge and passion for gardening, so you will soon find yourself surrounded by people who love this hobby as much as you do.

After all, there's nothing better than a common interest that brings people together!

But, before you proceed, you must understand that gardens are not just places where you can grow your food. They are special spots that have to be nurtured with much care and thoughtfulness.

Now, since you know why it's good for the earth, your family, friends, and yourself, let us get into some fun activities!

Chapter 1: Gardening basics

It might seem like an easy-to-do activity, but nothing could be further from the truth. There's a lot you need to learn before starting a garden, and this chapter will explain all of that. Soon enough, you'll become a green thumb everyone loves!

What does it mean to be a kid gardener?

We already discussed in the introduction what gardening is. But to be called a kid gardener, you must become a responsible, caring, and attentive person.

You must also know what plants need to grow well. Finally, remember that you can always get help if there's something you don't understand.

So, let's start with what plant needs?

A plant needs water, soil, sun, and air. The point is that regardless of the sort of plants you'll be cultivating, they will always require these three basic elements in addition to any other elements. Sunflowers, for example, can develop in almost any type of soil, but their blooms will be larger if the ground is well-nurtured.

On the other hand, if your flowers can't get enough sunlight, they will grow weak and be less attractive. But don't worry; you'll find out how to deal with any situation as you read on.

What is the best way to start your first garden?

Start with Location Hunting!

Before deciding what place is best for starting your garden, think about these things and make a note of your answers.

- **What do you want to grow?**
- **How much time do you plan to dedicate to gardening?**
- **What kind of garden style do you like?**

Now, depending on the size of your future garden, try thinking about these details you can use an adult's help as well:

- **Whether it's big or small?**
- **Is there enough sunlight for all the plants?**
- **Does the soil need improving to make it more suitable for growing?**
- **Does the garden have access to water?**

Once you've settled these details, you can start planning out your garden.

You can also pick a location in your house for gardening indoors. The only difference between indoor and outdoor gardens is that when it's cold outside or when there's not enough sunlight, you'll have to provide the right conditions for your plants yourself.

What are some common beginner gardening mistakes, and how to avoid them?

The first mistake people make when starting a garden is growing too many types of plants at once. That's why it's best to start with one or two kinds of flowers or vegetables. If you try to take care of all the plants at once, you'll just get confused about their needs, leading to failure.

The second thing beginners do wrong is not preparing the soil for growing. The soil can be too dry or too wet, and that's why it has to be improved before planting anything there.

Wet soil is hard to improve, so sometimes it might be better to start the garden somewhere else.

The third thing to avoid is not giving your plants enough water or air. Some plants can grow in dry soil, but others need it to be moist at all times. Paying too much attention to one type of plant won't hurt, but you can easily forget about other things like water since you're busy with other plants.

Now that you know what a plant needs in order to grow, it's time for you to choose the perfect flower or vegetable type for your garden. After all, when starting out, you can't always make mistakes; this section will help you pick well!

What to plant?

A plant can grow either from seed or from a cutting. Seeds are usually smaller in size, but they take much longer to grow into plants.
On the other hand, cuttings are larger and easier to get started with. There are also other things like bulbs, tubers, and corms which are all different types of embryonic plants that start growing when you add water and go through the process of sprouting.

Plants can be divided into the following three categories-

➤ **Annuals**

These plants will thrive for a year, after which they will perish.; they are best for beginners or for people who don't have much time.

➤ **Biennials**

They take two seasons to mature, so it's better if you can dedicate the proper amount of time to them.

➤ **Perennials**

These plants last longer than the other two types, and they don't perish at the end of the season.

Plants from seeds

These plants can be started in a small container with soil, and you benefit from them when they're mature enough to be transplanted.

You should know that there are eight different types of seeds, which are Baby seeds, Creole seeds, Edible seeds, Flower seeds, Fruit seeds, Vegetable seeds, Hybrid seeds, Improved seeds.

- **Baby seeds-**

They're a type of seed that has been altered so that the plant stays little after it sprouts. The seeds are also excellent for eating since they're soft and tasty.

- **Creole seeds-**

They are indigenous seeds, which have not been modified, at least not artificially. This implies that they are the plants' natural offspring, harvested after their blooms were pollinated.

The greatest thing about them is that they adapt quickly to your region's conditions.

- **Edible seeds -**

These seeds can be eaten and, as a result, are produced for that purpose. There are many edible seeds: pistachios, walnuts, corn, oats, sesame, pumpkin, chia, rice, etc.

- **Flower seeds -**

Flower seeds come in a variety of shapes, sizes, and textures. That is why you must pick the best seedbed for them to have adequate room to grow.

- **Fruit seeds-**

There are many types of fruit seeds as there are many types of fruits. Mango, watermelon, apple, grape seed are just a few examples.

The majority of the time, the plants that produce them are grown in orchards; however, with sufficient space and knowledge, you can grow some of them in your garden as well.

- **Vegetable seeds-**

These seeds produce plants that are cultivated for their edible fruit, stem, leaf, flower, seed, and root. They all need constant humidity to germinate, as well as heat; therefore, they're sown in the spring.

- **Hybrid seeds-**

These seeds are developed by crossbreeding two different plants whose qualities are desired in the offspring plant. As a result, they might be more resilient, produce more fruits and seeds, and resist insects and illnesses.

- **Improved seeds -**

This category includes seeds cultivated by humans through a series of methods and processes in a controlled environment.

They have several advantages since they will sprout plants better adapted to the environment.

Plants that will be easier for beginners if grown from seed

Tomatoes- They can grow in all kinds of soil, and they don't need too much sunlight. You can also get seeds that are hybrids or heirlooms.

Carrots- They usually take around six weeks to start showing up in your garden, which makes them a great choice for anyone who doesn't have time to tend the garden every day.

Lettuce- it's good for growing in both containers and on open ground; it only takes two weeks to see results in your lettuce plants!

Flowers- like marigolds, nasturtiums, calendula, sunflowers, and pansies can grow from seeds, and they only need 5 to 6 weeks.

Herbs- like basil, thyme, sage, parsley, and lavender can all be grown from seeds.

Cucumbers- they're perfect for people who don't have much free time to care about the garden regularly since they can grow in just three weeks.

Plants that are easier to grow from cuttings

These types of plants are best grown using a cutting or a bulb instead of seeds. This is because they are larger and more mature when you get them, so it's easier to transplant them after getting them started. Plants from cuttings are bigger than seeds. They reproduce by rooting after you place them in the soil and water them regularly. There are four types of cuttings: Softwood cuttings, Herbaceous cuttings, Semi-hardwood cuttings, and Hardwood cuttings.

Plants that will be easier for beginners if grown from cuttings

Mint- All it takes is a 3-inch piece of stem, and it will grow roots within seven days. It does well in small pots as long as it receives enough sunlight (at least 4 hours per day).

Roses- these plants reproduce from cuttings that you take from a previous plant. You will need a strong stem, and it's best if the leaves are still attached to the cutting when you put them in the soil.

Lavender- it's best to plant them during the start of spring. You can take a 2-inch stem and plant it in a container filled with rich soil that is also well-drained.

Scented geraniums- 12 inches tall can be made from a cutting, which will need to have its leaves removed beforehand. They're perfect for containers or for growing indoors in pots that are exposed to lots of sunlight.

Pine trees- They can easily grow from cuttings because all you have to do is stick the cutting into some moist soil, wait for it to sprout roots, and then transplant it wherever you want.

Herbs- like basil, parsley, and thyme can all be grown from cuttings because they're perfect beginner plants; you only need one week before the roots will start to form!

How should I prepare the soil?

As mentioned before, there are different kinds of plants; each one requires specific care depending on the kind of soil needed to start growing properly. Therefore, knowing what type of soil your plant prefers is the key to a successful garden.

Plants that prefer sandy soil

These plants can grow well in dry and warm conditions, and they need plenty of sunlight, too. Some examples of plants like this include sunflowers, zinnias, annuals like poppies, dianthus, cornflower, and cosmos.

Plants that like loamy soil

They make great pets for those who don't have much time because they can grow really quickly; some examples are foxgloves, snapdragons, carn (you should place them in moist soil), and campanulas (they can grow in cooler conditions).

Plants that prefer clay soil

These plants should be planted in full sunlight, and they should also have a constant supply of water so that their roots can grow properly. You can choose annuals like a wallflower, pansy, primrose, bee balm, and sweet pea; perennials include lavender and chrysanthemum.

Salt tolerant plants

They should be planted away from the sea because they need fresh water. When you buy them from the market, look for the ones marked as salt-tolerant to make sure that your garden will be great no matter where it's situated. Some examples are tomatoes (they need plenty of moisture) and petunias (they grow in small spaces).

Plants that, can tolerate dry weather

These seeds should be planted close to the ground, but they should also be left in moist conditions; some examples are poppies, cornflower, evening primrose, and foxglove.

By following these simple steps and choosing the right plant for the right type of soil, you'll be able to enjoy a successful garden filled with gorgeous flowers and vegetables!

Before that, let's dive deep into understanding the tools you would require to work on gardening.

Know your tools and materials required for gardening

Pots

To start gardening, you will need some pots. Depending on the size of your plant, you can choose a small pot or a big one; make sure that it has room for growth because if the soil becomes too dry, then the roots won't be able to grow properly, and they might end up dying!

Seeds or cuttings

As discussed before, not all plants need to be grown from seeds. You can also grow a plant from a cutting! Choose your desired type.

Watering can

This will help to keep your garden moist, especially if you're planting flowers or vegetables. Make sure that you water them daily so that they can develop strong roots!

Compost

Compost is made from organic waste, manure, or other material that can make the soil richer. Manure comes in many different varieties, and you can choose the one that fits your garden best! It's very important to make compost early on because it will be used as the plant's food source.

Soil for indoor plants

When you buy soil for indoor plants, make sure that there's little or no sand in it; even though this type of soil is really good for growing most types of plants, if your plant prefers sandy soil, then mix some organic matter into the potting mix before planting.

Tape measure

For measuring out how much soil you will need.

Plant labels

These are a great way of keeping track of your garden and a fun way to mark the plants you have there.

Hoe

A hoe makes it easier to work with your soil and evens out hard dirt so that the roots can spread more quickly.

Gardening gloves

To protect your hands from dirt and bugs, it's a good idea to wear gardening gloves. When choosing them, keep in mind that heavy-duty ones are best for shrubs or for handling spiky plants. To protect your hands from dirt and bugs, wear some gardening gloves.

Garden fork

Also known as an "awl," this tool is used to dig holes for seeds of new cuttings; you can choose how big the hole should be depending on the size of the plant!

Trowel

This item is a smaller version of a garden fork used to dig small holes and also for weeding.

Spray bottle

The process of spraying non-chemical pesticides such as soap, oil, or vinegar solution (1 teaspoon in 1-liter water) will help the plants develop their natural defenses against pests without harming them. Keep in mind that organic methods take longer, but they are ultimately better for your plants and garden.

Spade

You'll need it for cutting back roots and mixing compost into the soil.

Rake

This tool is mainly used only in the garden, so you should use it if there are some dead leaves on the ground, stones, etc.

Sieves

They're used in order to separate the lighter gravels from the heavier soil in your garden. You can also sift organic matter if needed!

Pruning shears

These are useful when you need to prune bushes or trees. You can buy them in different sizes depending on how big or small your project is.

A fork

Garden forks are used for turning over the soil and breaking up larger clumps of dirt. You should buy a lightweight one because it will be easier to use when working in smaller spaces.

Wheelbarrow

This is perfect if you don't want to carry loads of dirt on your own; wheelbarrows allow easy transportation of materials without straining yourself too much!

Gardening scissors

They are used for cutting away dead plant materials, cutting twine, and so on. This tool is also handy for picking up fallen leaves or even pinecones!

Gardening Diary

Keep track of your garden projects so that you can keep improving them!

These tools will help you weed your garden and prepare the soil for planting. They're really simple to use; you just need to push them into the earth and pull out the weeds. Keep in mind that you should wear gloves because some of these tools can be sharp!

Now that you know your tools and have your favorite plant ready for planting, it's time to take care of it! In the next chapter, you'll read about what to do each day as a gardener. It's as easy as one-two-three once you get the hang of it!

Chapter 2- Getting started

The practical work requires good preparation and a bit of effort. Your garden prompts you to get your hands dirty but also gives rewards! I will help you through the step-by-step process. If you do everything right, the reward is tasty fruit and veggies for you and your family.

All you need is to take care of your plants, and they will be very happy!

Every day is different, but there are some things that you need to do regularly.

But, before getting started with practical work, remember the most important thing is safety.

So, **Safety first!**

Here're the safety guidelines you must follow while gardening-

Thoroughly examine your site of the garden

Take the help of adults and inspect the area for any poisonous plants or insects and take notes of their location in your gardening diary. Ensure that the soil is not contaminated with harmful chemicals or septic waste and take care to avoid such hazards.

Choose a safe source of water

Your municipal water is usually a safe bet. Irrigate your edible garden with a potable water source. Have the water you're using tested for bacterial and other sorts of contamination on a regular basis if it comes from a private well or an untreated surface water source, such as a pond or river.

Your local health department can help you locate testing facilities.

Do not use chemicals

Never use harsh chemicals as you might harm yourself. Always try natural ways for fertilizers and pesticides. You can easily make it at home by the following method-

Mix 1 teaspoon of salt in a liter of water and put it into a spray bottle; mix the same amount of baking soda with two teaspoons of dishwashing soap and vinegar (use white vinegar as it's acidic). Spray this solution on your plants as this will stop pests from eating their leaves!

Choose the appropriate tools

Handle them with care to avoid injuries. Since hand power is used, it's important that the tool is lightweight enough so that you can work comfortably without hurting yourself. Wearing gardening gloves made from sturdy material is recommended while using tools. Sharp objects such as secateurs for pruning shears should be used under adult supervision, and you must remember to put them back on the shelf after use.

Remember

Do not leave your tools out in the rain or sunshine, as it can cause rusting and eventually damage them. Take good care of your garden tools so that they last longer!

Be extra vigilant with manure

Even though manure is a natural fertilizer, it can have pathogens in it, which can cause you to get sick. It is best to apply manure around established plants in the fall, as they are less susceptible to infection. Always use gloves when you are working with any fertilizer or manure.

Always have adult supervision

Most of these activities are simple enough, but you should not forget that there are chances of injuries because of the tools involved. So, always have a person who is more experienced or aged supervise when you are gardening.

Dress properly

Wear long pants, closed shoes, and gloves while gardening. You'll need to protect your hands from dirt or bug bites! You can also wear insect repellent or citronella oil which is very effective but try not to use it too much because it can be harmful to plants. Wear hats and sunscreen to avoid sunburns.

Personal hygiene

Remove all clothes after gardening and take a bath. Wash your hands regularly when you are gardening. Don't eat or drink with dirty hands! Clean your clothes worn during gardening.

Know when not to garden

If you are sick, do not go near your plants. If you are taking medicine, consult with your doctor if it is safe for gardening before you begin. Health always comes first! Also, don't work outside if the climate is too harsh; listen to your adults when they refrain you from gardening.

Follow your parent/carer's advice

Gardening is a wonderful hobby, but you should always listen to adults. They have done this before, and they can guide you with proper methods.

Be safe!

Always read the instructions on the product label before using it on your plants or in your garden! Gardening can be fun for all ages; just be sure to prioritize safety over everything else!

Now that you know all about gardening safety precautions. Let's dive to,

A practical guide for planting.

First of all, check the daily forecast and plan accordingly.

You can grow plants at any time in a year but remember that certain veggies have the preferred season. When the weather is favorable, start with pruning- it helps in the better growth of shoots and fruits or vegetables.

In summer, weed out the garden so that its roots don't disturb crops. Check the soil frequently to ensure they're moist enough but not wet enough. Finally, keep inspecting for pests on a regular basis!

Time to plant

As you know all your tools and gardening information, you can start planting. Choose the type of plant you want to grow and research their specific requirements; use the information provided in the first chapter. The number of plants depends upon how much sun or shade they need. Follow the guidelines that come along with the seeds; it's important to be precise!

Plant them at the right depth and space, depending upon their development needs. Dig a hole in the middle of each pot or on the ground with an appropriate depth. Fill the hole with soil mixed with manure or compost for fertilizing your plants.

Start small as they can get big over time.

Mix fertilizers after reading instructions

Mix fertilizer with water according to the instructions on the packet. Pour this mixture at the base or root of your plants or vegetables/ crops very gently, never directly! You can use compost tea for better growth results.

Water regularly

Maintain humidity levels around the soil by watering them daily- not too much or too little! It's easier to prevent weeds than to remove them after growing, so make sure you weed out every week or whenever needed. Watering helps in the removal of dead tissues from vegetables/ crops, so water is very necessary for growth.

Remove weeds when you see them

Weeds are unwanted plants that can inhibit growth or spread diseases to your crops. Whenever you see them, remove them by pulling the roots gently so as not to damage nearby plants.

Check that plant is getting enough sunlight

Regularly check that crops are getting enough sunlight. They need at least 6-8 hours of sun every day to grow well! For indoor plants, you need to be extra cautious! In case they're not getting enough sunlight, you can place them in a sunny window or near a bright light.

Stay positive and be patient!

Stressing about gardening is not going to help, so keep a positive attitude and enjoy the process of making your backyard garden better. Growing veggies or plants take time, effort, and patience that will all lead up to a wonderful end product! Never lose hope if a plant does not yield as expected because there's always something good around the corner!

Are you ready for harvesting? Bring in your harvest by storing them the right way!

Harvesting

To harvest veggies like cabbages, cauliflower, and broccoli, cut off their florets or flowers, respectively. Cut plants near the base so the plant itself can regrow next season! You should shear vegetables like carrots or radishes instead of cutting them as they tend to recover quickly, unlike others.

Harvest fruits like grapes, berries, etc., after their color change from green to bright yellow/orange/red, which means they're fully ripe and ready to eat!

Pick fruits and vegetables when they're ripe

Harvest them before the ground freezes, or it may rot. You can check the soil temperature to know if frost is coming. Place harvested vegetables/fruits in a cool and dry place like a basement, shed, etc., where humidity levels are low and ideal for storing veggies!

Store apples, stone fruits, and other fruit by laying them on a table covered with newspaper sheets. Grains should be stored in an airtight container which you can buy from any home improvement store.

Remember that excess moisture should be avoided while storing veggies as it causes rotting. Be patient till the next growing season! The best time to start gardening is directly after winter ends, which means it's time to plant new crops again!

Now that you know the overall process let's make a weekly routine to help you plan better once the initial planting is done.

Days of the week and time to work in your garden

You can follow these instructions for each day of the week:

Monday: Weeding and pruning

On Monday, it's time to get started with weeding and pruning. Weeds absorb nutrients from the soil, which can harm your plants, so remove them as soon as possible! Cut branches or stems at the base instead of pulling them out by their leaves so that the plant remains intact. You can also use a sharp spade or hoe to cut through weeds easily.

Tuesday: Planting new crops/seeds
Seeds are available in packets that come with complete instructions on how to plant them. You can sow seeds directly into the ground or start them indoors. Make sure you know your area before planting new plants!

Wednesday: Fertilizing and harvesting
Water your plants every day so that the soil is moist enough for good growth! It's time to feed plants with fertilizer if required; watermelon requires lots of nutrients, so apply compost at the base of its stem every week after it starts flowering. Finally, harvesting time comes, which means gently removing vegetables/fruits from their stem or roots respectively. Remember not to damage nearby plants while harvesting!

Thursday: Make compost
Composting is necessary if you want to make your soil nutrient rich. To learn how to make compost, you should refer to these instructions carefully-
1- First, you need to collect all the compostable materials in your house like eggshells, burnt toast, etc. Please make sure they're dry but not too dry!

2- Next, put these compostable materials in a bucket or bin with holes at the bottom so air can pass through easily. Add water if necessary, during this process! You can add dried leaves or grass clippings for better results.

3- Then, cover the bin/bucket with a lid and leave it outside in direct sunlight for several weeks. This way, bacteria inside create heat that is required to break down items into rich soil!

4- Finally, when everything breaks down into thick black matter, then it's ready to use in your garden.

Friday: Protect plants against pests and diseases

Pests like aphids or snails attack plants by sucking out their nutrients which leads to wilting of leaves and other problems. Plant disease can be prevented by spraying them with fungicides! You can find many organic solutions at hardware stores, so check there first for fungicides before buying one online!

Saturday: Relax and enjoy the fruits of your labor

After each week comes to an end, take some time to relax and enjoy what you've accomplished so far. You can visit your plants daily, look at the weather and anticipate the upcoming week's plan!

Sunday: Go shopping and rest

It's time to go shopping for new gardening supplies like tools, saplings, etc., if required. Remember that low prices should always be preferred as expensive items don't necessarily provide better results than cheap ones.

And you deserve some time to relax with your family and friends. You can enjoy your meal or just sit around in the garden during this day- it's up to you!

Apart from this, some things should be done regularly,

What to do each day as a gardener

Keep an eye on plants and trees. Ensure that all your plants are healthy and safe for gardening. Plant any seeds or bulbs you see! Maintain records of what you planted, when they were planted, and where. All this information can be helpful later when you decide to harvest them.

Keep the surrounding areas clean and remove damaged leaves and branches as soon as possible. Trash can be used, but don't burn them as they release toxic gases! If you see weeds, pull them out carefully by their roots.

Water your plants at least once a day to make sure the soil is moist enough for good growth. It is also important not to let too many nutrients run away with water runoff or accumulate in the form of fertilizer or manure salt deposits at the base of plants, known as fertilizer burn.

I am sure by now you must have understood how to be a gardener and must have enjoyed learning about it!
As we become master gardeners, let's move towards creating beautiful theme gardens. The next chapter will help you create a beautiful garden with themes that you wish to have!

It's time to surprise people with your creativity!

It's time to surprise people with your creativity!

Chapter 3: Theme Gardening

Theme gardens are a type of gardening that allows you to create a garden with a certain theme of your choice. A themed garden can be made by adding essential components like plants, sculptures, statues, rest-houses, waterfalls, ponds, fountains, and ponds.

Theme gardens not only look beautiful but also provide you with a serene environment in your backyard or garden, perfect for relaxation and outings!

Before creating a themed garden, first select the theme of your choice, whether it's indoor or outdoor! Then, considering your space available, you can plan how much area is required for each component.

For example, if you want to create an indoor garden, you have more control over where plants are placed because the size of indoor spaces is limited, unlike outdoor gardens with vast areas without boundaries. Therefore, designing an indoor garden will require more thought and planning than that of an outdoor one!

However, even if it's designed well, be ready for some required maintenance for indoor gardens as they need proper sunlight, so plants don't die easily. Compared to this, the maintenance of an outdoor theme garden needs less than anything that fits the theme. The best part about the themed garden is that it makes your garden look like a one of a kind!

Theme gardens can be created for different themes depending on the person making them and their interests.
I will share some of my favorite ones-

Fairy Gardening theme

Aesthetic: This theme is suitable for all weather conditions and can be placed anywhere indoors or outdoors.

Plants: Tiny-looking plants like ferns, lavenders, baby's tears, etc., are good for this themed garden as they look fairy-like!

Decorations: Look for tiny pots, thrones, maybe some colored butterflies to decorate the garden.

Process: Ensure that the space available is near a window or if you want it to be indoor, place it in any corner of your house. Create a square or rectangular-shaped garden and start planting flowers. Use stakes to give support if required. Put tiny pots at 4 points, where the square meets diagonally, and finally decorate with small thrones.

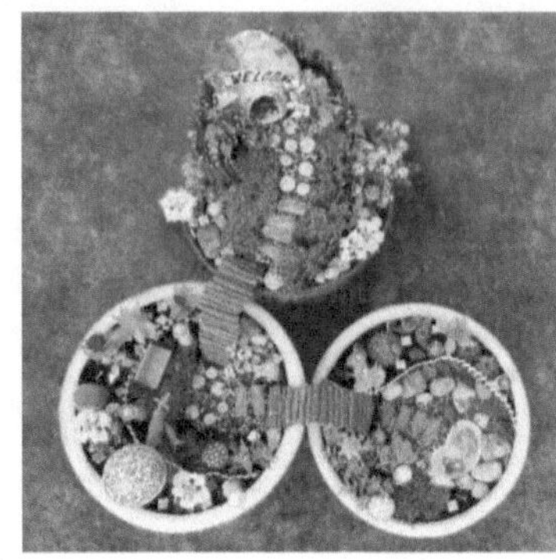

In addition, you can add small cottages, pagodas, or houses made of natural materials like wood and stones with some tiny furniture inside. Small plants are required for this themed garden as they look perfect in these kinds of gardens. To decorate the garden, use small pots, tables, and chairs at different points, or even a small pond can be added if space allows. Decorate with tiny boxes and colorful butterflies!

What to expect: A fairy garden will make your house look like a home of little fairies or people who wish to live in one!

Play Gardening Theme

Aesthetic: This theme is suitable if you like playing in your garden. The garden can be created anywhere, indoor or outdoor, and is good for all weather conditions.

Plants: Depending upon the kind of play you want your garden to look like, select the plants accordingly. For example, if it's a playhouse, then you can use small flowers with some grasses! On the other hand, if it's an adventure-themed kid play garden, use wildflowers with small trees! Choose fast-growing plants, vines, creepers, etc., for this theme. You can also use edible plants that are relatively faster growing, like strawberry, corn, etc., along with some lovely flowers that are brightly colored!

Decorations: Sculptures look perfect in play gardening themed gardens. They can range from small to large depending on the space available. Apart from sculptures, you can also add swings or seesaws or even a see-saw table! You could also make art forms of animals using recycled materials like clay pots, toys, etc. if you wish to do so.

Process: Start by giving your ideal shape to the garden, whether it is circular, triangular, rectangular, or any other. Once you have given your shape, start adding edible plants as they grow fast and keep the garden looking fresh all year round! Then add some flowers according to your chosen theme and finally place a plant of choice where the path leads. Leave a good amount of space for the play activities to take place.

What to expect: A play gardening themed garden will bring out your adventurous side, making you live life on the edge.

Butterfly Gardening Theme

Aesthetic: This theme is suitable if you like butterflies and will look perfect when placed outside.

Plants: Only plants that attract butterflies should be used in this themed garden because the sole purpose of this themed garden is to provide a habitat for butterflies! So avoid using plants like vegetables or corn in the butterfly-themed garden. You can choose from a range of colorful flowers that attract butterflies. Some safe places to add them are- Hibiscus, Sunflower, Marigold, etc.! Not just flowers, even some other plants like water lilies and grasses look fabulous along with these beautiful flowers!

Decorations: Statues like fairies, gnomes, butterflies are perfect for this theme. Add them wherever you can! Also, add houses, benches, etc., where butterflies may land on!

Process: This theme requires a lot of patience as you cannot simply create your garden overnight or in one day. Start by creating habitats like piles of leaves, flower pots with some grass and leaves on them, logs, etc. You can also create your own habitats for butterflies! Plant some flowers that attract butterflies and wait for a few weeks. Once the plants start growing and look healthy, add some more of such plants. Your garden is ready when you see butterflies fluttering around!

What to expect: A butterfly-themed garden will attract lots of beautiful butterflies, which will make your garden look like a place of magic.

Shoe Gardening Theme

Aesthetic: This is my favorite theme as it makes gardening very interesting for kids and adults alike! Themed gardens can be created anywhere indoor or outdoor and are good for all weather conditions. It gives boho vibes to your garden, making it look unique and quirky! It's a space-saving theme and can be created in any corner of your house. This themed garden is good for all weather conditions.

Plants: Use small to medium-sized plants in your themed garden. You can use climbers or creepers for decorating purposes. Fill in any gaps with grasses and wildflowers too. For this themed garden, choose small flowering plants that suit your shoes/boots size. Suited plants for this themed garden are those which create perforated leaves like parlor palms, rubber plants, etc., as they look like shoes!

Decorations: Look for polished stones, tiny pots, thrones, maybe some colored butterflies to decorate the garden. Remember, not all gardens need a lot of decoration as they give a natural vibe! On the other hand, if you wish to make your theme stand out, then do add some extra flair using figurines, doors, etc., along with plant lighting at nighttime!

Process: The only thing that's important while creating a shoe-themed garden is making sure the plants selected are small and can easily be placed in pots/containers. The containers used should be of all shapes and sizes. You may even add some broken pottery or ornamentation like tiny boots, shoes, etc., or any other creative idea of your choice!

What to expect: A shoe-themed garden will give your home a boho vibe along with making you feel creative inside out.

Tropical porch Gardening Theme

Aesthetic: This theme is perfect for outdoor summers and is unique due to the tropical plants added to it! There's nothing more refreshing than enjoying an evening on your porch with a cooling breeze! This theme requires a large open space as it will give you lots of options to decorate the garden.

Plants: Use small-sized plants/shrubs which can give an amazing feel to your porch! Fill any gaps using grasses and flowers too! For this theme, avoid using big plants as they generally take up all the space! Some safe plants for this theme are- Pothos, Heartleaf Philodendron, Fiddle Leaf Fig, etc.

Decorations: For this themed garden, create its own unique decorations like colored ferns, spiky plant spikes, etc. You may also use some other accessories like water features along with plant lighting for an evening delight! In addition, add some extra porch swing or hammocks to make your porch feel even more luxurious!

Process: To start this themed garden, ensure you have an open space. Then create two partitions using palm trees planted in large pots with slow-growing plants/shrubs on the sides. This will give a perfect tropical vibe to your garden. You may plant some vine flowers along with small grasses for decoration purposes too! Remember to always place the big plants at the center while placing smaller ones on the sides!

What to expect: A tropical porch garden will fill you up with freshness, and its bright colors will lighten up your mood instantly! Plant lighting at night time adds a magical feel to it, making you forget all worries of life!

Mini pizza gardening Theme

Aesthetic: This theme is perfect for all seasons and is unique due to the mix of veggies, fruits, etc. In this themed garden, use decorative pizza slices as a partition and plant ingredients of pizza. The best thing about this themed garden is that it can be created indoors as well as outdoors making it a versatile theme!

Plants: You can use veggies, herbs, and fruits used in pizza-like bell peppers, basil, etc. Fill any gaps using grasses and flowers too! For this garden, choose small size plants that look like toppings on your pizzas! Some safe plants apart from pizza ingredients for this themed garden are- Aloe Vera, Coleus, Miniature rose, etc.

Decorations: Creating unique decorations is the key to making a mini pizza-themed garden stand out. Try adding figurines of veggies, cheese slicer, knife, pizza cutter, which will make your garden unique in itself. You may also add some other accessories like tiny pots with herbs used in pizza or miniature pizza slice statues along with plant lighting for an evening delight!

Look for some statues or figurines to give an artistically appealing look to this theme. Decorative items like pots in different colors with matching plant labels make your garden look attractive.

Process: For this themed garden, you will need a partition that can be made using decorative pizza slices planted in pots/containers. Make sure that you place taller plants on one side while placing smaller ones on the sides! If there are any gaps, plant grasses or flowers to fill them. Fill in with some colorful butterflies and accessory stones like a heart-shaped paw print, etc., for added attraction.

What to expect: Mini pizza-themed garden will give your home a modern feel along with making you feel fresh inside out! Add some pizzazz to this theme by using decorative items like colored pots etc. A mini pizza-themed garden will instantly give a true Italian pizzeria feel to your home as all the ingredients will be fresh!

Potato time tower Theme

Aesthetic: This is perfect for all seasons with its good cultivation rate! Create a tower of hay along with some decorative stones to make your garden stand out. Plant vines at the base of the tower.

Plants: Potatoes, ornamental grasses, colorful flowers.

Decorations: Add some small ornaments like rocks or figurines or other such creative things to add interest to the theme. Use plant lighting during the nighttime if you wish to

illuminate your head! Fill in gaps with moss and stones to give your themed garden a natural feel.

Process: Find potatoes that have healthier skins since these will be more durable than their sprouting counterparts. After that, construct your tower. Cover the potatoes with about a foot of hay and dirt mixed together by lining the tower's edges with hay. You must maintain your potato crop covered, or you'll grow green, poisonous potatoes as it grows. Because the structure is more exposed to the air, keep it well-watered throughout the growing season. You can use a few cute containers to create a tower instead of using hay. You can also use decorative stones or any other creative things you wish to add interest to your garden.

What to Expect: Potato time tower-themed garden will give you fresh potatoes along with the opportunity to show your creativity! Decorate this theme with colorful pots and vines at the base. A potato time tower garden will make sure that your mood is instantly lifted!

All the theme gardens are beautiful if you put effort and creativity into them. Experiment as much as you like, and don't be afraid to use your imagination. You can try different themes and see which one suits your space and mood!

Take help from any one of your family members or friends if you need it. Just make sure that you ask them for advice and not their whole time; you must do it yourself.

A garden like this will help you grow even more artistic with your creativity and imagination. It will enhance your skills and give you one more reason to love gardening.

So, go ahead and plan your own garden or themed garden to enhance your inner green thumb!

I hope you have selected your theme, and let's start your green garden!

Chapter 4: Green Garden

Green gardening is all about using sustainable practices to produce food. It can also be defined as a system of agriculture that takes care of the environment and soil fertility.

You have to use natural fertilizers or compost from your own leaf litter and garden waste rather than chemical fertilizers in this kind of gardening. Using a good organic mulch at the base of plants is also a very important green gardening practice for retaining moisture in the soil and preventing weeds from growing around cultivated plants.

Green gardeners believe that only healthy soils support healthy plants, which ultimately provide high-quality, healthy food products that are free from chemicals sprayed on them.

When you start with green gardening, there is no end to it; it's an ongoing process that needs constant attention, especially until you get to the point where you don't have to keep checking on your plants every day.
You might be thinking,

Why prefer Green gardening?

Green gardening has multiple benefits for both the environment and the people eating the food produced.

Environmental benefits of Green gardening are:

• Biodiversity thrives in a garden where chemical pesticides are not used, meaning that you have more insects, birds, butterflies, and other wildlife in your green garden, which can positively affect our ecosystem.

• Pesticides release toxic chemicals into the air while green gardeners use mulches which retain moisture in the soil and keep it cool, stopping evaporation. They also help heat up soil at lower levels so plants can grow well, even during winter.

• Chemical fertilizers are harmful to bees because they are attracted to them, making plants produce pollen with altered DNA, linked to collapse disorder (CCD)in bees. Green gardens don't use any kind of chemicals, and so there is no danger of pollen with altered DNA being produced.

• Chemical fertilizers contain salts that accumulate in the soil as dead spots that can become difficult to grow anything on these areas later on as they don't retain water and nutrients effectively.

• Organic matter such as compost, leaf litter, and mulch eventually break down into humus, providing a natural source of nutrients for plants instead of chemical fertilizers.

The Health benefits of green gardening are:

• The food we eat from a green garden is pesticide-free and has great taste because it's not sprayed with chemicals during its growing period or after harvesting, as only the nutrient-rich organic matter was used to maintain its growth.

• Food from a green garden is free from chemicals and is also more nutritious as it has been grown using organic fertilizers, which provide additional nutrients to the plants.

• Chemical fertilizers often contain high levels of nitrates which can be hazardous for human health too if consumed in high amounts. However, organic matter does not cause the accumulation of nitrates in the soil, so there's no chance of consuming something harmful for our bodies.

Now that we know its importance, let's learn how you can create your own green garden.

How to create your green garden?

You can create your green garden by using mulch made out of coconut husk, cocoa shells, composted leaves, and other waste products. This will ensure that nutrients are re-used in the soil while keeping weeds away.

Using organic fertilizers is another great way you can go green when gardening. In addition, regularly adding layers of leaf litter at the base of growing plants is a great way to recycle organic wastes.

You could also make your own compost bin or container to recycle your kitchen waste into high-quality fertilizer, which you could spread around among all your plants!

These are some simple ways to start going green with your gardening, and soon, you will start seeing the results with your own eyes!

Here's a step-wise process of creating a green garden-

1) Dig a small pit and place some coconut husk and cocoa shells in it.

2) Place this container wherever you find space, preferably near the plants that need care more often, such as tomatoes or potatoes.

3) Cover this with leaves and add another layer on top every few days to create layers of mulch.

4) Add kitchen wastes such as vegetable peels, eggshells, etc., between these layers. This will help all the organic matter to decompose quickly into humus which is beneficial for plants.

5) Use organic fertilizers made at home using ingredients mentioned earlier in the article to fertilize your plants during their growing period. This will ensure that they are getting nutrients from an organic source rather than chemicals.

6) Save money while shopping at home by using the seeds you get from your harvest or even use saved seeds from previous harvests if they are still feasible!

7) Rotate your crops every year while growing things together that fix nitrogen into the soil, creating almost no need for any added nitrogen fertilizers!

8) Use a variety of plants so in case certain kinds don't do well in a particular season, other kinds will take over in their place without requiring any further work from you since they all have different needs!

9) Harvest your veggies and fruits when they are ready to eat! These will taste much better than vegetables and fruits from the supermarket because you don't need to worry about any chemicals since you used natural fertilizers throughout their growth period.

10) Have fun while gardening and learn about environmental impact, healthy eating habits, and growing food at an early age!

You will soon have a green garden to love and cherish as you become clear about the green gardening process. But, to achieve it even more easily,
Avoid these common mistakes as a green gardener:

- Avoid using chemicals to produce food that can harm you and the environment!
- Not recycling waste products around your plants.
- Avoid gardening in a space without providing water for plants at regular intervals.
- Not reading up on different types of fertilizers which can be used as per plant requirements.
- Constructing a garden where rainwater cannot reach it easily.
- Allowing yourself to get overwhelmed by trying to go green all at once instead of taking small steps towards it at regular intervals.
- Forgetting about mulching and using specific fertilizers with desired nutrients for healthier plants and soil! (Remember: "Prevention is better than cure")
- Not thinking about the weather conditions before planting specific plants as some of them require a lot of Sun while some others need shade.
- Not doing enough research about organic fertilizers and their availability in local markets near you!
- Using too much or too little water- can be harmful to soil and plants.
- Not using mulch regularly to build a sustainable green garden.
- Planting new grass on top of existing soil where there is no grass growth which will result in dead spots forming with time! Remember: "Grass helps clean up certain toxins."
- Not supporting local nurseries and shops that sell organic fertilizers, composts, or other types of mulch/mixtures helps create a sustainable green garden.

- Not providing enough shade for your plants to survive during the summer months.
- Not re-using existing mulch or leaves/plant material that is decaying into compost.

As you progress with your sustainable green garden, you can add decoration and use terracotta pots or containers of different shapes and sizes to create a wonderful piece of art for yourself.

Your creativity knows no bounds when it comes to gardening so let's see what you can create for yourself.

Meanwhile, let's have a look at my favorite garden arts.

Chapter 5: Garden Art

There are many kinds of garden art that you can make to decorate your theme or green gardens. Your garden art can be as simple as a couple of pots and planters with vines and plants running down the side, or it can also be complex, like a furniture piece you would like to use for your seating!

Both kinds will make your gardens look prettier and will help you express yourself better. You can paint or draw anything that inspires you, even people's faces if that is what you wish for.

For example, if you like birds or any animal, in particular, paint their images on your pots and planters. Your imagination is the only thing standing between you and your garden art!

So go ahead and begin making your garden art, starting with things that are easily available at home. Then, you can either paint them yourself or ask someone else who has a good painting hand to do it for you – no matter what happens, your garden art will surely look pretty.

How to Make Garden Art?

Making simple garden arts like pots decorated with vines and plants is not as hard as it seems; all you need is a little bit of creativity and effort. As long as the piece has some relevance to gardening, go ahead and experiment!

Here is a list of some interesting garden arts and crafts which I love; along with methods to create them:

1. Hanging Planter

Use hangers to attach empty glass jars with the help of strings so they don't fall on the ground. Place them in different corners of your garden space but make sure to place them at least 1 foot apart because the idea behind this art is for each jar to produce its fresh herbs or vegetables independently without having any competition between plants!

2. Horse Stable Herb Garden

This is probably a unique type of garden art out there! If you have a space where you can place it, this is something you should try. It's also perfect if your theme happens to be western or has horses playing an important role in it. You can even use old buggy wheels and other rustic elements to make this piece of garden art, which will look very interesting once the plants are done growing around them!

3. Doll/Toy Art

Another terrific idea for garden arts and crafts is attaching toys to planters with the help of hangers so that they don't fall below. Toys like dollhouses, teddy bears, etc., look adorable when hung up on hangers attached to different parts of your garden space.

4. Animal Figures

You can attach animal figures with the help of hangers to planters or pots in your garden to make it look attractive! Animals like frogs, turtles, etc., are very cute and will definitely make an interesting outdoor art piece for your gardens. You can even paint their images on your garden's sidewalls if you have enough space to do so.

5. Flags/Flags Art

Flags will be a great idea for outdoor arts and crafts if your theme is about countries or sports. You can choose flags that represent different countries or teams that influence the theme of your green space, so it becomes more celebratory when needed! Make sure this art piece also has plants growing around it because happy plants make happy gardens!

6. Human Art

This is another very interesting garden art idea for creative people with a green thumb. You can use old wooden crates or pieces of paper and draw images of children on them, which you then cut out. Now, these mini images should be attached to empty jars that will serve as planters with vines growing around them! This way, your images grow progressively into more complex forms thanks to the plant life surrounding them. Finally, they become what they love to do most – gardening!

7. Recycled Bottle Herb Garden

Old, recycled bottles are among the best things you can use for making garden arts and crafts because they're so easy to find around us. You just need to cut off their bottoms then place them upside down into soil-filled pots or flower beds. Once they start sprouting, plant herbs inside of them like rosemary, basil, fennel, parsley, etc. Just pick the ones that grow well inside small spaces like this one!

8. Bicycle Tire Planters

Bicycle tire wheels are one of those garden arts and crafts ideas that take up little space but pack a lot of charm once they're done making them. You only need two bicycle tires per piece which you then hang from raised structures like beams or boards attached to the side of your garden walls. You can then plant seeds among them and watch as they grow into a beautiful green, flowery piece of garden art!

9. Rustic Garden Signpost

Making garden arts and crafts from new items is fun but recycling old stuff is even more interesting. That's why this rustic signpost idea might be one you need if you have a lot of materials lying around at home that could be restored to become part of your outdoor arts and crafts collection. All you need here is an old wooden board with metal plates on which you can attach letters that say different friendly messages for passers-by – things like "Welcome," "Garden Rules," "Don't touch the plants," etc.

10. Flower Painting

If you're a big fan of paintings and arts in general, this flower painting idea might be your thing. You obviously don't need to paint a whole garden wall for this purpose but small portions or spaces here, and there will do just fine. Just create paintings yourself that have flowers growing around them, so the piece becomes more vibrant when it comes to color! Your creations can look similar to modern art if you want to meet both old-school traditions and new-age concepts at once!

11. Vintage Treasure Boxes

Old vintage treasure boxes are an ideal addition to any garden that's colorful enough because they have their unique charm. They become part of the overall aesthetics, especially if they're made from metal with little keyholes on them! In addition, you can plant different flowers or herbs that grow into pots then put them on top of the treasure boxes, so they bloom nicely when an onlooker approaches.

12. Monochrome Checkered Garden Wall

This garden art idea is all about making your green space look more fun and modern. All you need is to get a huge, checkered piece of paper, preferably cut out from cardboard because it's durable enough for this purpose! Now, paint the whole thing using black-and-white colors so that one side has painted squares while the other simply remains white. Once it dries up, attach the thing to your garden walls with adhesive materials like glue or double-sided tapes. Then watch as passers-by stare at it with curiosity!

13. Garden Flags

Garden flags are among those arts and crafts ideas that take up little space but have a tremendous impact! All you need is to paint different drawings on different fabrics – one of which must be waterproof if possible – then stick them onto sticks or wooden poles that you stick into the soil right next to your plants. They'll start being flapped by wind, giving your garden an even more lively look!

14. Tin Can Planters

If you're still not getting enough from these easy arts and crafts ideas, this garden tutorial will be perfect for you because it involves tin cans! All you need are some big metal containers which you can easily cut in half with scissors before making holes on their lower sides.

Once all of them are ready, put soil inside them, then plant whatever seeds or seedlings that grow well into small spaces. You can paint the cans in different colors if you like, making them stand out even more!

15. Hanging Garden Baskets

This garden art idea is one of those that involve both creativity and simplicity at once. All you need are some big metal baskets which you can easily find in junk shops or simply make yourself by covering up wire mesh with fabric. Then, put soil inside them before hanging them on trees or walls around your garden, so they act as containers for plants like ivy. Another version of this idea is to plant all kinds of climbers on thick ropes to create a vine-like system that entirely covers an old wooden beam above your outdoor space.

16. Reclaimed Window Planting Boxes

Remember how we told you that you could find all kinds of interesting materials in junk shops? That's definitely the case with these window planting boxes! All you need is to place old windows on their backs then cut small holes around them. Once they're ready, plant different seedlings inside before hanging them from walls or fences using thick rope or chains. The best thing about this idea is that it looks incredibly stylish and will even be a great addition to your porch's look!

17. Hanging Pot Garden

Liven up your garden by adding several large metal pots filled with soil and different plants! All you need are some sturdy chains or ropes along with hooks. Attach them to either side of your garden's fence, making sure each one is in the middle, so they don't touch the ground! Also, make sure to use non-toxic paint so that all of these details won't be dangerous for anyone who goes inside the yard.

18. Painted Wheelbarrow

When it comes to backyard garden arts and crafts ideas, this one is definitely among the unique ones because it involves an old wheelbarrow that can be painted in various colors. Once done, fill its tray soil, then plant flowers or herbs inside it before pushing it around your outdoor space. If you don't have a wheelbarrow, this idea can obviously be adapted to a regular cart or a suitcase instead.

19. Personalized Art

Are you looking for more unique garden arts and crafts ideas? Well, these personalized pots are what you were looking for! All you need is to use old containers – plastic bottles work great here – then give them personal touches by writing names on them using paint or stickers. Plant whatever seedlings or small plants that grow well near the soil surface before hanging each pot from walls, doors, or fences with adhesive tapes. This will all liven up your garden incredibly!

20. Hidden Treasures

Here's one more idea for those looking for backyard decorating ideas: make small hidden treasures with different layers containing soil and plants inside them! These will look great along fences since they're nicely hidden from view when you're outside! Simply place old boxes or containers on their sides, cut small holes in them then plant different flowers and seeds inside before covering the top with soil.

21. DIY garden wind chimes

Turn old spoons into beautiful garden wind chimes in just a few easy steps. You'll need some silver spray paint, rope, and some old spoons with their edges filed down to avoid any harm. Spray-paint the spoons, then tie each one onto the rope to create an enchanting noisemaker that will liven up your backyard!

22. Painted Rocks as labels and decoration

These painted garden rocks are simple to make and will look great around your yard. You'll need some rocks that you can find in most yards, Mod Podge, acrylic paint, and rubber gloves (if you're using real glitter).

For this project, I like the idea of using rocks as labels for each plant container. Because let's face it; who remembers what's planted where? Let alone keeping up with watering! All jokes aside, these painted rocks would also make great borders or little stepping stones throughout your landscape beds. What do you think?

23. DIY Outdoor Chalkboard

A DIY Outdoor Chalkboard Wall is an easy way to expand the use of any outdoor space. You can use it as a menu or just jot down little notes to remember what needs doing when you're in the yard, like "turn on sprinklers" or "start weeding." It's especially helpful if there are multiple gardeners using the space because everyone will know what needs doing when!

24. Recycled Watering Can

Why buy a new watering can when you have so many things to recycle in the house?! You just need an empty milk jug or any other container that has a spout on its top, so you're set! Once it's done, just water whatever plants you're growing. This activity is super fun and educational too!

25. Mess-Free Bird Feeder

An old plastic bottle is all you need for this activity. Cut off its top, then poke some small holes on it before turning it into a bird feeder! Fill the bottom with birdseed, turn it upside down and place it outside to attract birds. This is one of those garden arts and crafts ideas that teach us about nature and how to respect and take care of animals.

26. Mailbox Garden Art

You can easily turn an old metal mailbox into a beautiful garden art to label where each plant comes from. All you need is some fabric or wrapping paper, then paint it with colorful scenes that show what's planted there, like sunflowers, for example. This will be super helpful if you are growing food in the backyard!

27. Garden Art with Pebbles

Turn your garden into an art gallery by creating a stunning piece of wall art that will decorate the entire outdoor space. All you need are some old jars, paint, and rocks! Simply fill them up with colorful pebbles before painting their lids to create beautiful jar garden art. After it dries out, just attach the lid back on each one of them to see your finished artwork.

28. Flower Bed Stencils

Make learning about flowers even more fun by turning flower beds into stencils! The best thing about this idea is that you can create as many stencil designs as there are types of plants in your garden! This way, every single plant bed will be unique. How to do it? Cut out flower shape stencils from thin cardboard, then simply place them where you want to draw next.

29. String Art

Making simple string art is one of those ingenious ideas that will teach you basic crafting skills while decorating the garden. All you need is wooden boards, nails, and some colorful thread. You can use nails to hammer the thread into place, then simply hang it up on a fence or wall! Don't forget to take help, so you don't hurt yourself.

30. DIY Wind Spinners

Spin your yard into a beautiful garden with these DIY Wind Spinners! You'll need some old CDs along with paper and fabric scraps. Simply cut out flowers and other shapes from

different colors of paper before gluing them onto the discs, then paint as desired before hanging it up outside on some twine or rope

All the garden art and craft are pretty if done with love; just try to use available items rather than buying new stuff. Don't forget to take the assistance of adults when you are dealing with sharp and dangerous tools and materials. Now that we have our garden ready, it's time to enjoy it thoroughly!

Chapter 6: Enjoying your Garden

You may be worried about the fact that your garden is not perfect. It can be a little messy, or it may look too barren. Don't worry, just because it doesn't have flowers that you love right at this moment doesn't mean it won't have them soon!

All gardens go through distinct changes as different seasons pass by and knowing what to expect from each season will help you better enjoy your garden. You should also know how to maintain a clean and healthy garden so it can yield good results every time.

That's why harvesting is one of my favorite activities!

It's always fun picking vegetables like carrots that have been under the ground for months on end. Or maybe you're growing some tasty strawberries that would be great on top of ice cream!

No matter what it is, harvesting will be one of the best parts of gardening. As you pick your fruits and vegetables, you get to enjoy your fresh produce.

It's also time to plant trees so they can start growing for next spring.

Some tips for enjoyable harvesting:

- Harvest early in the morning or late afternoon.
- If you're harvesting squash, wait until the fruit is fully mature and picked at its peak.
- Pick cucumbers when they're young and tender.
- Be careful with picking tomatoes because they are harder to grow than many other garden vegetables.
- Pick your fruit and vegetables early in the day, so if there is any bruising, it will be less noticeable on the surface of your produce.

- Harvesting makes you feel more connected with nature as well as the fact that every day spent in the garden yields new fruits and vegetables, which are fresh, healthy, tasty foods. So, enjoy the process.
- The best advice I can give you on harvesting is to be patient! If you plant something, wait until it's mature enough to pick. You'll know when it's ready because everything comes with its unique look or appearance.
- Also, with harvesting, you don't want to pick everything at once because if you leave some vegetables on the plant, they will continue to grow and provide more fresh produce later in the year when it's time for your garden to sleep during winter.
- Documenting the harvesting process will be a rewarding experience. It's important to always take notes on your progress because nothing is ever for certain!
- That's why it's good to keep a garden diary. It will help you remember which plants did well last year and how much effort you should put into them this time around. You don't ever want to forget about the small details because that one detail might be what makes or breaks your harvest.

In the end, what you'll get from all of this hard work is an abundant harvest that can feed your family and fill your pantry with fresh food. But you should also store your harvest properly.

How to store your harvest properly?

Different fruits and vegetables have different requirements.

Storing root veggies is quite simple; keep them in a cool, dry place where the temperature won't go over 50 degrees Fahrenheit.

Coolers are also great options for keeping your vegetables fresh. Just make sure they don't already have food inside them, so you don't contaminate your product with another plant's smell or taste!

Herbs like basil and sage can be stored by stem wrapping with tissue paper or in airtight containers with dampened (not wet) peat moss.

Tomatoes need to be kept away from cold air at all times because it will cause them to stop ripening which means no more juicy tomatoes for you unless you want to eat them green! Some people put tomatoes in a warm area and surround it with black plastic, but hanging them upside down is the best way to store them.

When harvesting vegetables like cucumbers, leafy greens, and herbs, it's good to harvest with scissors rather than tearing at the harvest with your hands or pulling at it.

If you're harvesting beans, don't forget to pick off the flowers so they'll keep growing more of those tasty treats we all love!

Finally, when selecting an area for storing fruits and vegetables, make sure that whatever place you choose keeps out pests like mice and insects like beetles and ants because they can ruin your harvest. Always check your produce for visible signs of infestation!

One of the most important things you can do when preserving your fruit and vegetables is to keep them out of the sun. If they sit under direct sunlight, they'll start to rot. It's also a good idea because the sun's rays contain some pollutants that will emit toxins into your produce if left in its light too long.

The last thing I want to tell you about harvesting is never waste anything! Even if it seems like nothing more than a tiny sprout or a branch that doesn't have much on it, every part of the plant has a purpose, whether for food or medicine.

The leaves might turn brown, but as long as there isn't any mold growing on them, just compost them and use them as fertilizer for next year's garden.

Every bit of plant has the potential to be food if you know what you're doing, so don't throw anything away!

Some ways of spending your best time in the garden and watching it grow!

One of the best ways to spend your time in the garden is by watching it grow! There are a lot of different things you can do if you have cultivated your garden.

- You can lay down in the grass and watch the clouds go by or pick flowers from your garden to make into bouquets.
- Another way to spend time is by taking care of bees so they can pollinate your plants or hunting for earthworms which will help with soil fertility.
- Make time for your friends and family – invite them over and grill burgers or steaks by the bonfire! They'll love spending time with you in your garden.
- Spend some time to plan out next year's layout. While also enjoying the weather while it lasts. Spending time and making memories with friends and family by hosting cookouts or grilling outside; also taking advantage of sunny days by relaxing outside, laying out with your outdoor furniture, playing games like ice skating, tobogganing, or sledding. Have gratitude towards nature for being able to enjoy outdoor space throughout the year.
- The break between seasons is a good opportunity to make sure everything is prepared for the next season.
- Make time to plant new annuals and perennials and order new seeds before the growing season starts.
- You can also dedicate time to pruning plants before the growing season starts.
- Sometimes it feels great to kill some time by making some compost for your garden; then, you'll be able to order new seeds or get them from the local plant store.
- It can also be fun to take advantage of windy days or where only brave hikers venture out by taking walks under the moonlight. Feel closer to nature while being one with it.
- As you get more experienced, you might consider getting a greenhouse so everything will keep growing even when it's snowing outside.
- Spend time journaling the current garden and creating a garden diary to look back on in the future.
- It's a good idea to take support and guidance from adults around you for creating your gardening community by joining or hosting a meetup with fellow gardeners; building a strong gardening community will raise support and encouragement for you throughout the seasons. You can also take your guardian's help in joining online forums or local gardening clubs to help each other out and share your knowledge about plants and animals that grow well in your region.

- Another thing you should consider is creating a scrapbook so family and friends can follow along on your progress.

There are plenty of other ways to spend quality time in your garden. However, the most important way to enjoy your time in the garden is harvesting anything that you might be growing at home!

Enjoying Springtime in Your Garden

Spring is one of those seasons where everything begins – new life, fresh blooms, and warmer weather!

Even though your garden may have lost its color during the winter, it will be ready to blossom again when spring arrives. The warmth of the sun helps tender plants break through the soil when you can finally see patches of greens emerging in your garden.

You can also expect to see many flowers in this season. Some of the most common signs that spring is arriving are when trees start sprouting leaves, early-bird chirping wakes you up in the morning, and when you see your garden turn bright green before your very eyes!

Knowing what to plant in your garden during this time would be a good idea so you can properly take care of them.

Enjoy this season by planting your flowers, veggies, and herbs. You may also want to add some new trees and shrubs that you feel would benefit your garden or yard.

Springtime is a great time to enjoy gardening and all the things that come with it – spending more time outdoors, enjoying nature, trying out gardening projects, etc.

Enjoy spring in your garden by doing different activities with friends and family, such as yoga, painting, and even making a bird feeder!

Water games are also a great way to spend your time in this season. Have fun by pouring water on each other!

Your garden will also receive more sunlight during spring, which means you should plant flowers that thrive in these conditions.

Have fun planting tulips, daffodils, roses, and snapdragons!

You can also begin pruning your fruit trees so they can bear better yields the following season. You may also want to start mowing your lawn or applying fertilizer on it if it needs some refreshing.

Enjoying springtime is all about enjoying the nature that surrounds you. Spend more time with your garden, and it will give back to you in many different ways!

Enjoying Summer in Your Garden

Once the spring season begins to settle out, you'll be able to see your garden come alive with all sorts of colors and blooms! So, enjoy the milder weather by planting flowers that are native to warm climates.

Enjoy this season by hosting activities like picnics or barbecues! Your garden is the perfect place to host these events because it can provide you with various settings, each one offering its unique charm.

For instance, you can set up an outdoor dining table that overlooks your garden or set out some lawn chairs near a koi pond under a willow tree.

In addition, you should know that the most important thing to consider during this season is watering. Even if it doesn't look like your garden needs water, make sure to check on it every day. You should test moisture levels using a finger – when you can easily press into the soil without resistance, then it's fine!

Finally, keep an eye out for bugs and insects in your garden because some plants attract them more than others. If you spot anything crawling around, simply get rid of them by spraying insecticides or other types of solutions over any affected areas.

Enjoying Fall in Your Garden

When fall rolls around again (which isn't very long since summer goes by quickly), there are several things you can do to make the most of this season.

First, rake up all the fallen leaves, so you don't have to deal with them later. They are great for your compost pile or mulch around your plants because they will help retain moisture in the soil. Plus, they'll keep weeds from popping up!

Next, it's time to prepare your garden for winter by laying down some wood chips or other protective materials across the base of each plant. Doing this will protect any tender new growth that may come up during springtime.
You should also wrap evergreen trees and shrubs tightly with burlap because their branches are used to staying warm year-round.

Enjoy this season by bringing in your outdoor furniture and lighting some candles or warming lanterns to set the mood. Arrange them around your fireplace or place where you can gather with friends and family! It's time to embrace everything about autumn – drink hot chocolate while strolling through the garden, toast marshmallows while enjoying dessert by the bonfire, or just simply relax under the sun.

Finally, don't hesitate to pick some flowers before they wilt because this is when they're at their best quality. As long as you cut them off right above a node on the stem, they can be enjoyed indoors.

Enjoying Winter in Your Garden

Winter is a reprieve from the busyness of the spring and summer months. During this time, you can work on planning next spring's garden layout or simply enjoy some quiet time in your outdoor sanctuary. Winter is a beautiful time to enjoy your outdoor space, but it can be quite challenging too! It's cold and wet, so all you really want to do is curl up next to the fire with a hot cup of tea or cocoa.

But before winter settles in for good, there are a few things that need to be done before you can officially start enjoying it. Usually, around November is the best time to plant trees because they don't require as much attention as other plants do. When planting evergreens, make sure to have them face south so they'll get plenty of sunlight during the peak growing season!

Finally, decorate your garden with all sorts of string lights so it looks festive year-round. You can also sled adorn poles with garlands made out of holly leaves, so everyone knows the holidays are coming! Also, you can break out the ice skates and grab a toboggan for those cold days when it seems just right to go tobogganing.

Enjoy this time of year by bringing out your holiday decorations and playing some festive music as you sip hot cocoa. Then just sit back and enjoy the serenity as snow drifts down from above!

The garden can be enjoyed at any season.

Spring brings new growth and life to plants after a dormant winter, it also brings weeding, pruning plants before the growing season starts, and getting to work in your garden. It allows you to enjoy the weather while it lasts.

Summer brings harvesting flowers, enjoying the garden with friends and family, grilling outside, or hosting cookouts, taking advantage of sunny days by relaxing outside, and laying out with your outdoor furniture.

While fall brings raking leaves into the compost pile or for use as mulch around your plants.

Winter gives you time to plan for next spring's layout, enjoying quiet time in your outdoor sanctuary, planting trees, decorating, and playing festive music as you sip hot cocoa or play games like ice skating, tobogganing, and sledding.

With this, our beautiful journey reaches a conclusion! I am sure you enjoyed reading it as much as I enjoyed writing it.

Leave a 1-click review!

~

I would be incredibly grateful if you take just 60 seconds to write just a brief review on Amazon, even if it's just a few sentences.

https://www.amazon.com/review/create-review-asin=B09ML9VJCF

Conclusion

Gardening is not just for growing food; it is also a science that helps improve lives by reconnecting people with nature. Whether you have a green thumb or are just starting out, gardening is a rewarding and time-honored tradition that everyone should experience in their childhood.

A child who actively enjoys gardening will have a better connection with the food they eat and will be more prepared to take care of their very own garden as adults.

They will also find that organic gardening is a lot of fun and could easily become a hobby or even a career option as they grow older.

It's an opportunity for you to develop your green thumb, and it's also a chance to grow healthier produce for your family and friends.

This e-book has shown you how to gain the necessary knowledge and skills to start your own garden and be successful every step of the way. It's going to be your companion rather than a one-time read.

There's no need to spend all day in front of the e-book; you can learn and try the methods simultaneously, then learn more and implement them further. You can learn at your pace in your own time in the comfort of your home.

Utilize the knowledge given in this e-book to have the best garden ever, not just for yourself but also for your family and community.

Remember, practice makes perfect, so keep taking notes and keep iterating until you get it right. Whatever happens, never give up because even mistakes can turn into great rewards with enough effort. There is much more to gardening for kids than just producing food; it's also about caring for our natural resources.

It takes patience and practice, so don't get frustrated if your plants don't grow the way you want them to. Keep learning more about how they work so you can become a true gardening genius!

A failure is only a failure if it isn't followed by success; always keep that in mind when something doesn't go your way because there's always room for improvement! Even if what you did was an honest mistake, learn from it and keep going because you'll never know if something will work unless you try it out.

Soon you will realize that gardening is a hobby for life!

It teaches you to take care of your surroundings while also teaching you patience, perseverance, responsibility, and more. It encourages healthy eating habits by teaching you where food comes from and how easy it is to grow your own food.

Gardening requires some upfront work (choosing which seeds or plants one would like to grow) with long-term benefits (harvesting your crop). Be prepared to spend some time outside in order to reap the benefits.

You will be the sole caretaker of your garden. So, be sure that you are ready and willing to take responsibility. But don't let that intimidate or overwhelm you but also be prepared to learn as much as possible before getting started.

It will take some experience and knowledge in order for it to become successful; however, with learning and patience, it can be well worth it!

You are responsible for your own success, so make sure to always read up on how things work before implementing them into practice. Believe me, taking notes is very beneficial because every time you do something differently, write down what happened so you can better understand what's going on.

The most important takeaway from this e-book is that in gardening, you'll always discover something new to learn and try, making it an endlessly fascinating experience.

It is also comforting to know that even if you aren't the most natural-born green thumb, there's always room for improvement as long as you keep learning more about plants.

Never give up on your garden because mistakes can turn into great rewards with enough effort and patience. Above all, don't forget to appreciate what we have and conserve whatever we can because nature is precious.

This ebook is my special gift to you. I have added my experience and tricks from my personal gardening journal. You can use it to inspire yourself, family members, and friends through education and action. Sow the seeds of knowledge so those good things may grow within your community, nation, and beyond! It will help you in uncovering the secrets of successful gardening.

My advice to you is to enjoy what you are learning and know that anything is possible with determination, practice, and the right information. Gardening is not a task but rather a way of life. It's about caring for our earth, our environment, and most importantly, it teaches you to take responsibility for what you are doing!

I'm glad we undertook this journey together because now you're ready to begin your own garden with the proper tools for success! Whether it's for food or just to add beauty to one's life, Gardening is a rewarding experience. If you enjoy nature, this ebook will be a great starting point in your gardening journey.

You must also ensure that you work with nature, not against it. Refrain from activities which damage or pollute the environment. Practice sustainable gardening practices that help the biodiversity and production of healthy food.

Most importantly, keep trying and never give up because every day is a chance to start fresh! Now you can refer back to this e-book while planning your next gardening session and make sure it's an enjoyable and fruitful one.

Don't forget to enjoy yourself as you cultivate beauty, health, and prosperity!

Now go out there and get your hands dirty!

But before you go, please share a review on Amazon so that other children can also discover the secret to your gardening success.

My other books you will love!

Amazon.com/dp/B09MLBKYFS

Amazon.com/dp/B09ML9VJCF

Don't forget to grab your GIFT!!!

http://daphnemcooper.com/parenting.pdf

Joining the PME Community

Looking to meet other parents that can help you on your parenting journey? If so, then check out the Parenting Made Easy (PME) Community here:

https://www.facebook.com/groups/293830159257919/

References

- Types of Plants

Types of Plants: Annual, Perennial and Biennial | Teleflora Blog

- Growing plants with stem cutting.

Plant Propagation by Stem Cutting | Types of Stem Cuttings (ugaoo.com)

- Tools for Gardening

Gardening for kids : Tools to get them started - Kids n Clicks

- Theme Gardening.

Gardening With Kids Using Themes - Gardening Know How

Kids Gardening: Tips, Ideas and Projects | Planet Natural

Down to Earth : Garden Secrets! Garden Stories! Garden Projects You Can Do! By Michael J. Rosen. Harcourt Brace, ISBN: 0152013415.

- Garden Art

kidzkorner - ICanGarden.com

Garden Crafts for Kids: 50 Great Reasons to Get Your Hands Dirty. By Diane Rhoades. ISBN: 0806909994.

Learn to Grow! The Fun of Gardening For Children (gardenforever.com)

www.ingramcontent.com/pod-product-compliance
Lightning Source LLC
Chambersburg PA
CBHW021129070726
47591CB00014B/1865